Teaching language and study skills in secondary science

For Michael

Teaching language and study skills in secondary science

Lesley Bulman

HEINEMANN EDUCATIONAL BOOKS

Heinemann Educational Books Ltd
22 Bedford Square
London WC1B 3HH

LONDON   EDINBURGH   MELBOURNE   AUCKLAND
SINGAPORE   KUALA LUMPUR   NEW DELHI
IBADAN   NAIROBI   JOHANNESBURG
PORTSMOUTH (NH)   KINGSTON

ISBN 0 435 57085 4

Typeset in 11/12 Sabon
Printed and bound in Great Britain by
Biddles Ltd, Guildford and King's Lynn

Contents

1 Introduction

This book has been written for all practising science teachers. Its main aim is to give advice on how they can educate their pupils to become autonomous learners. Education seen as the transmission of knowledge from teacher to taught is very limited—we as teachers cannot know all the answers to our pupils' questions and when they leave school they will not have the benefit of a team of teachers providing them with information. Our most important function as teachers is to teach our pupils how to learn on their own. Learning how to learn involves the acquisition of skills, some very simple, some extremely complex. Pupils without these skills, after leaving education, will become bigoted, rigid and, finally, ignorant.

The Bullock report (1) in the 1970s initiated the movement towards whole-school policies for language teaching. However, the HMI secondary survey in 1979 found that this concept of whole-school planning has not been adopted in many schools, and had been implemented in even fewer. (2, p. 102)

This book gives advice on how a science department, in isolation if absolutely necessary, can progress towards developing language and study skills in its pupils. This isolated approach is not ideal and it is to be hoped that a successful programme in the science department would encourage other subjects to follow suit and become eventually a programme for the school.

Chapter 2 discusses the relationship between the aims of science and language and study skills and includes a full list of skills as an appendix. Chapters 3-7 focus on different language skills and how they can be improved. Chapters 8 and 9 are concerned with study skills and the final chapter is a section on how and when to teach all of these skills. Most of the chapters in this book are divided into three sections: an introduction, a discussion of the problems, and strategies for coping with the problems. The section on problems is rather more theoretical and draws on research and surveys as well as my own experience. This section is intended to encourage practising science teachers to look more closely at their work in the laboratory. The strategies I outline are mainly examples drawn from my own experience and from other sources. One theme that runs through each chapter is that teaching study and language skills cannot be prescriptive. A wide variety of techniques needs to be demonstrated and practised so that pupils may find combinations that suit their own learning style.

Many science teachers may ask 'why teach these skills in specialist lessons when there is so little time to teach the subject itself?' There are many answers to this question, but undoubtedly the most telling reason is that by improving these skills in our pupils we will improve their understanding of science as well as increasing their ability to learn more about science. Scientific language—its vocabulary, style of writing, complexity of the concepts embodied in words—poses an enormous hurdle to a pupil's understanding. If we can help pupils cope with the language difficulties then they will be more able to understand the scientific concepts.

Many classes in science are in mixed ability groupings (over a third of all secondary schools have mixed ability first year classes (3)). If pupils are to learn in these classes successfully they must become independent as learners. Even in the fourth and fifth year many science option groups include pupils of a wide variety of abilities and if they are to succeed in examinations pupils will have to work at very different speeds and levels.

Examinations and methods of assessing pupils are changing towards a greater emphasis on course and project work. With this change, a pupil's ability to find, use, and communicate information will be assessed alongside their scientific knowledge and skills.

Science teachers have been worried that girls opt out of the physical sciences and that this has an extremely restricting effect on their choice of careers. One reason amongst the many that have been suggested is that girls enjoy and are good at using language skills and that these skills are often considered to be unnecessary in science and certainly given less status than mathematical or practical skills. If this balance was redressed then girls might begin to become more interested in physical science.

Many science teachers may feel that the teaching of language and study skills is valuable—and that they are already being taught successfully in science lessons. A major survey carried out by the Schools Council project on the Effective Use of Reading provides little evidence for this.

These are the percentage time allocations for different activities during the science lessons they surveyed. (4, pp. 108–22)

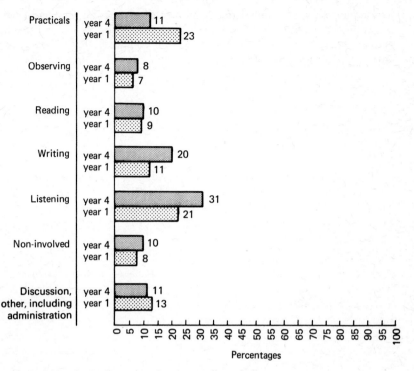

(i) Activities observed were not always mutually exclusive.
(ii) Other activities observed included administration, calculating, and deliberating.

Further analysis by Lunzer and Gardner of the time spent reading showed that 93% was done in under 30 second bursts—there was no thoughtful, continuous reading. By far the majority of time spent in working was in copying. (More details of this report and a lot more discussion is given in Chapters 3 and 4.)

It seems clear from this survey that in the majority of science lessons language and study skills were being neither taught nor used. The case for teaching language and study skills relies on the importance of learning these skills and the benefits these skills will bring in increased understanding. Although some science teachers may be aware of this and are teaching these skills, by far the majority of science teachers are not.

David Merlin and Paul Buck writing in *Starting to Teach Study Skills* end with this:

'Don't be put off by colleagues who cynically regard study skills as the latest 'bandwagon'. The importance of learning study skills is painfully obvious. None of us can rely on old knowledge in today's world. Only by helping pupils to become adaptable to whatever situation they find themselves in, can we fit them for whatever the future holds. Unlike facts, skills are flexible, thus study and information skills could well be the single most valuable acquisition in a child's school career.' (5)

References

1 Department of Education and Science *A Language for Life* (Bullock Committee Report 1975)
2 Department of Education and Science *Aspects of Secondary Education in England* (HMSO 1979)
3 Department of Education and Science *Mixed-ability Work in Comprehensive Schools* (HMSO) 1978)
4 Lunzer E. and Gardner K. *The Effective Use of Reading* (Heinemann Educational Books for the School's Council 1979)
5 A. Irving (ed) *Starting to teach study skills* (Edward Arnold 1982)

2 The aims of science education and study skills

Some science teachers would see the aims of science education as completely divorced from any mention of study skills. Many more science teachers would see language and study skills as service skills for science—skills that can be assumed to exist in one's pupils as a result of the endeavours of the English department. Even when it becomes only too obvious that pupils are not deploying these skills, it is often seen as a failure of other teaching departments or of a pupil's intransigence. It is not seen to be within the province of science teaching because there is 'not enough time to teach these skills *and* real 'science'.' However, more and more science teachers are looking closely at the general aims of science teaching and realizing that if these aims are to be achieved, language and study skills will not only be essential tools but also on any list of objectives that could be drawn up from these general aims.

The aims of science eduction have been put most clearly in '*Alternatives for Science Education*' (1) and are repeated in '*Education through Science*' (2). They are:

(i) The acquisition of a knowledge and understanding of a range of scientific concepts, generalizations, principles, and laws through the systematic study and experience of aspects of the body of knowledge called science.

(ii) The acquisition of a range of cognitive and psycho-motor skills and processes as a result of direct involvement in scientific activities and procedures in the laboratory and the field.

(iii) The utilization of scientific knowledge and processes in the pursuit of further knowledge and deeper understanding, and the development of an ability to function autonomously in an area of science studies to solve practical problems and to communicate that experience to others.

(iv) The attainment of a perspective or 'way of looking at the world' together with some understanding of how it complements and contrasts with other perspectives or ways of organizing knowledge and inquiry, and without which the individual cannot achieve a balanced general education.

(v) The attainment of a basic understanding of the nature of advanced technological societies, the interaction between science and society, and the contribution science makes to our cultural heritage.

(vi) The realization that scientific knowledge and experience is of some value in the process of establishing a sense of personal and social identity. (2)

Any teacher who attempted to achieve these aims with her pupils without developing highly advanced reading and recording skills would simply not succeed. It is not possible to *transmit* to pupils such a science education—inherent in the aims is the belief in pupil involvement in their own scientific development. Aim (iii) is quite specific; pupils should be able to 'function autonomously' in their science studies. In order to do this pupils must be able to find, interrogate, evaluate, record information, and generalize from it—all skills that can be grouped under the title 'language and study skills'. This applies not only to science studies in schools but also to the work and studies of professional scientists who need these skills to be as developed as their practical skills. Handling written information is an extremely vital part of a scientists' task and one that has been woefully neglected in the past. C.P. Snow's article on 'the two cultures' is just as relevant today as when it was written over 20 years ago. (3)

Aim (v)—to obtain an understanding of the 'interaction between science and society'—cannot be transmitted from teacher to pupil, neither can it be learnt in practical lessons. It can only be done by much reading research, thinking, and discussion by the pupils.

The context of science education as outlined in *Education through Science* makes the point very clearly that science is not just a laboratory-based subject where the only information lies in test tubes and dissections but is such a wide-ranging subject that information has to be found second-hand in books and libraries, searched for and selected, before it can be useful to the pupil or communicated to others.

The three contexts outlined in *Education through Science* are:

(i) *Science as an intellectual discipline:* the pursuit of scientific knowledge as an end in itself which leads to an understanding of the essential principles and processes of science and allied disciplines.

(ii) *Science as a cultural activity:* the more generalized pursuit of scientific knowledge and culture that takes account of the history, philosophy, and social implications of scientific activities, and therefore leads to an understanding of the contribution science and technology make to society and the world of ideas.

(iii) *Science and its applications:* the development of an appreciation and understanding of the ways in which science and technology contribute to the worlds of work, citizenship, leisure, and survival. We would include under this heading an understanding of the way scientific and technological ideas are used to create and maintain an economic surplus, facilitate participation in democratic decision-making in a technological society, enrich and sustain a wide range of leisure activities and pursuits, and enable the individual to utilize scientific ideas and technological processes in the context of increasing self-sufficiency, the conservation of resources and the utilization of alternative technologies. (2)

This takes the study of science beyond laboratories, beyond science textbooks into everyday life: into television programmes, magazines, newspapers, the local environment. Pupils in science lessons must have developed skills to assess information, to find information in their local surroundings, to make decisions based on this information, and to communicate it effectively to others. It is with study skills of this kind that this book is concerned.

To many people the word 'skill' implies a mechanical activity that when perfected becomes almost automatic—like driving a car or doing a titration. Many science teachers may view study skills in this light and therefore see them as service skills necessary in order to achieve the higher plane of scientific thought. However, many of the skills identified as 'study' skills are not only as intellectually demanding as skills considered to belong to 'science' but are often only slightly different aspects of these 'scientific' skills.

The stages in generating a hypothesis are not very different from the stages a student must go through when starting an assignment. (The word 'assignment' covers a wide variety of tasks that teachers give their pupils to do. They range from the simple worksheet where single facts may have to be found, through essays, making of the pupil's own notes, to highly complex projects where the pupil is only given the minimum guidance over the choice and completion of the task.) These stages are outlined in the appendix to this chapter

and include:
—Focus on what is the topic and purpose of the assignment
  —Assess the pre-knowledge
  —Formulate the new knowledge required
  —Evaluate the accuracy and authority of a (written) source.

They are not very different from the stages in judging the accuracy of an experimental result.

If it is accepted that many study skills are similar in kind to scientific skills then pupils' science education will be improved by teaching these skills within their science lessons. This has been eloquently articulated by *T. Canick* in an article called *Bullock Revisited.*

'A teacher of science or geography, for example, whose concern is simply to impart facts to his pupils, who checks their absorption of these only by questions demanding short factual answers, who dictates quantities of notes without considering whether the vocabulary and structures he uses are intelligible to his pupils, who devises worksheets that take no account of his pupils' language competence—the problem with such a teacher is that he is using limited and ineffective methods of teaching science or geography. Good teachers of these and other subjects know that pupils learn and understand better if they are able to ask questions, to explore and discuss the matters presented to them, to sift and relate evidence, to speculate, to work towards conclusions, to bring ideas into full understanding by expressing them in their own words, while learning progressively how to express them in ways appropriate to the discipline of the subject.' (4)

One final reason for incorporating the teaching of study skills into science lessons, rather than in separate timetabled lessons or in a pastoral programme, is the widely-held view that these important skills are best learnt in the context of timetabled subjects such as science.

This view was first embodied in recommendation 139 in the Bullock Report:

'Recommendation 139: To bring about this understanding every secondary school should develop a policy for language across the curriculum. The responsibility for this policy should be embodied in the organisational structure of the school.' (5)

It is a main conclusion of the Effective Use of Reading project (6) and in Ann Irving's book *Educating Library Users in Schools* (7).

A whole-school policy for study skills has many benefits in that the skills are seen as being immediately relevant to the learning task of the pupil; through the acquisition of the skill, understanding of the subject will be fostered, and practice in the skills will be much more frequent than if study skills were a rare timetabled lesson or short course. It is also very clear that teachers are all too frequently setting tasks which do not allow pupils to develop active study skills—causing frustration to teacher and taught.

Language and study skills are not just essential for the education of our pupils, they are equally essential for their science education and truly represent what science teachers wish to achieve—an *education through science*.

Appendix

A list of study skills

Study skills can be grouped together in various ways: different teachers will make their own different subgroups because many of the skills are so major, so interwoven into subjects, that they are hard to disentangle.

I have grouped these skills under five main headings:

A Skills needed to complete assignments
(These relate almost entirely to written material.)
  1 Formulation and analysis of assignment
  2 Information skills
  3 Reading skills
  4 Note-making skills
  5 Essay and project-writing skills
  6 Evaluation
B Talking and listening skills
C Learning skills
(These emphasize the retention of information and not the initial understanding.)
D Organization of study
E Examination technique

A Skills needed to complete assignments

Many of the following skills will be needed even for the simplest assignment, and all, at a higher level, will be needed to complete projects.

1 Formulation and analysis of need
(a) *Focussing on what is the topic of the assignment, its purpose and audience.*

(b) *Assessment of time required and available.*
(c) *Assessment of pre-knowledge.*
(d) *Formulation of new knowledge required.*

2 Information skills
(a) *Numerical and alphabetical sequencing*
(b) *Use of subject index and catalogue*
    Ability to look up subject, retrieve Dewey classification number, and locate resources on shelves of library.
    Ability to understand and use information on catalogue card.
(c) *Use of contents page and index*
    Ability to use contents to locate appropriate chapter(s).
    Ability to use book index to locate page reference.
    Ability to select relevant passages from several references.
(d) *Use of reference books*
    Ability to use dictionary to look up definitions.
    Ability to use encyclopaedias including straightforward use of index and cross references.
    Ability to use atlases.
(e) *Use of written materials other than books*
    Ability to use periodicals, magazines, and newspapers to find information.
    Knowledge of the content, arrangement, and indexing of these materials.
(f) *Selection of resources*
    Ability to assess the scope, relevance, bias, accuracy, authority, and difficulty of a book by examining its cover, preface, index, notes on the author, publisher, and by sampling its contents.
(g) *Ability to follow up bibliographic references*
(h) *Ability to use public libraries*
(i) *Ability to locate other sources of information*
    Knowledge of range of sources available.
    Assessment of which sources are accessible.
    Assessment of which sources are appropriate.

3 Reading skills
(a) *Skimming of text* (or other resource)
    Ability to use contents page, headings, diagrams, summaries, etc. to obtain the main theme of a text, and its suitability and relevance.
(b) *Scanning of text* (when appropriate)
    Ability to read through passage quickly to locate specific references.

(c) *Reflective reading*
     Ability to retell main facts of a story/passage in own words.
     Ability to retell main facts of a story/passage in correct order.
     Abilities to summarize a story/passage with/without text orally
     and in writing.
     Ability to frame own questions on a text.
     Ability to use context clues.
     Ability to build vocabulary.
(d) *Variation and improvement of reading speeds*
     Ability to vary reading speed to suit material.
(e) *Assessment and manipulation of information*
     Evaluate accuracy and authority of source.
     Distinguish between fact/opinion
                         fact/fiction
                         relevant/irrelevant
                         essential/non-essential.
     Compare information from different sources.
     Relate new and old information.
     Make generalizations and conceptualize.
     Construct hypotheses and generalizations.
Use of other resources
Ability to assess pictorial and visual data for content, bias.
Ability to interpret mathematical and statistical data, tables, charts,
diagrams, maps, sketches.

4 Note-making skills
These skills are very closely related to reading skills.
(a) *Formulating questions to be answered.*
(b) *Titling of passages* (with justifications for titles).
(c) *Recognition of key-words, phrases, facts, concepts in sources
     and their selection.*
(d) *Use of abbreviations.*
(e) *Lay-out and presentation* (systematic and memorable).
(f) *Organization of data.*
(g) *Incorporation and interpretation of diagrammatic materials.*
(h) *Reassembly of written format from a set of notes.*
(i) *Generalize/conceptualize.*
(j) *Use of diagrams, flow charts, and maps where appropriate.*
(k) *Knowledge of when to copy, paraphrase, or summarize.*
(l) *Organization of material for easy access.*
(m) *Non-written recording*
     Ability to make tapes, computer programs, slides when avail-
     able.

5 Essay and project writing skills
(a) *Understanding of the different modes of written expression*
Awareness of the available modes of writing *viz.*, transactional, expressive, poetic.
Ability to use appropriate mode in relation to title and audience.
(b) *Posing of specific questions* (structuring of writing)
(c) *Selection of material*
For appropriateness, relevance, recognition of bias, justification of ideas, level of difficulty, discrimination of fact and opinion.
Pinpointing of information missing and return to search.
(d) *Structuring of material*
Ability to structure a transactional essay: introduction, development of main line through three or four main ideas (each with support and illustration), conclusion (answer to question posed, comment on topic, wider implications, further considerations).

In a project, the collection and selection of materials, note-taking, posing of questions, and the ability to perceive wider issues, modes of presentation (different styles of language, use of diagrams, charts, illustrations).
Selection of different structures in relation to the question: compare and contrast, debate, describe, etc.
Choice of sequence.
(e) *Writing*
Ability to write with conciseness, relevance, clarity, style, and adequacy to title.

6 Evaluation
(a) *Self-assessment.*
(b) *An understanding of the assessment of others.*
(c) *What has been learnt.*
(d) *How to improve.*

B *Talking and listening skills*

1 Listen effectively to speakers, ideas in formal and informal situations.
2 Express ideas, findings, impressions by conversation, discussion, or presentation with appropriate degree of formality or informality.
3 Participate in discussion by listening and contributing.
4 Evaluate arguments in discussion.
5 Ask and answer questions.
6 Give and respond to instructions.

C *Learning skills*

1 Organize notes for effective learning.
2 Learn actively, not just read.
3 Concentrate on one subject at a time.
4 Interrogate syllabus and past papers.
5 Identify learning goals.
6 Work out short- and long-term timetables for study.
7 Practice and repeat knowledge that is to be memorized.

D *Organization of study*

1 Understanding of problems of study
(a) Ability to analyse personal study difficulties.

2 Organization of time and place to study
(a) Ability to analyse how all available time is allocated.
(b) Ability to organize one's study time and a place for study.

3 Use of systematic study methods
(a) Ability to set definite goals for each study session.
(b) Ability to self-assess the effectiveness of the study timetable and the achievement of goals.
(c) Prior review/questioning before session and recall at conclusion of session.

E *Examination techniques*

1 Written examinations
(a) Allocation of time to questions.
(b) Read through examination paper.
(c) Ability to choose questions adequately and to work through the best to the weakest.
(d) Read and respond to key words in question (compare, describe, etc.).
(e) Use appropriate writing skills.

2 Multiple-choice questions
(a) Allocate time adequately.
(b) Use appropriate strategies.

References

1 Association for Science Education *Alternatives for Science Education* (ASE 1979)
2 Association for Science Education *Education through Science* (ASE 1981)
3 Snow C.P. *The two cultures and the scientific revolution:* the Rede lecture 1959 (Cambridge University Press 1962)
4 Canick T. 'Bullock Revisited' *Journal of Biological Education* Vol 16, No 4 (1982) pp 1–20
5 Department of Education and Science *A Language for Life* The Bullock Committee Report (HMSO 1975)
6 Lunzer E. and Gardner K. *The Effective Use of Reading* (Heinemann Educational Books for the Schools Council 1979)
7 Irving A. *Study Skills Across the Curriculum* (Heinemann Educational Books, Organisation in Schools Series 1983)

3 Reading

Introduction

Methods of teaching science have undergone many modifications in recent years and with these changes the place of reading has also altered, although reading has rarely played a major part in science lessons. Science teachers, in general, have not used reading as a way of developing pupils' understanding of science, but as a useful source of facts for answering homework and occasionally classwork questions.

It might be said that there are three main styles of science teaching: the traditional, the independent, and the 'Nuffield' style. Within the 'traditional' science lesson the main reading material was the standard class textbook. The teacher gave instructions for such practicals as were done by the pupils and provided the pupils with notes, either dictated or copied, covering all aspects of the subject. Pupils used the textbook for homework or for answering questions in class when their own notes were not sufficient. Pupils were expected to have the skills needed to read independently and to extract information, but did not need to read in order to understand because the teacher, who dominated the lesson, had already explained the scientific concepts to the pupils.

Nowadays, in mixed-ability groups the pupils are expected to work independently of the teacher, and worksheets often dominate the lesson, providing pupils with sheets of information for their practical work and with questions that the pupils must answer during and after the experiment. Many of these worksheets have as few words as possible. Some even give pictures of the apparatus and of each stage of the experiment. Reading is kept to an absolute minimum because the emphasis is on doing the practical work, almost to the exclusion of understanding the scientific concepts (1). These courses do not, generally, require books as sources of information. Therefore, although there has been an increase in individualized learning, there has also been a decline in use of a class textbook. If there are background booklets produced to complement these courses, they are often more illustration than text and would certainly not extend the fluent reader (2).

Only too often, in mixed-ability groups with poor readers we say that these pupils cannot read. We therefore decrease our demands on their reading to the point where they do not read and therefore they cannot read.

In the Nuffield science courses there is a great emphasis on practical work that is much more open-ended and leads to discussion. However, whether the discussion is pupil- or teacher-dominated, it rarely involves using books for explanations or evidence. Indeed books, being largely collections of very well-established facts, are an unwelcome antidote to discovery learning.

These examples show the exaggerated extremes of the three main styles of science teaching. However, there can be little doubt that reading plays a very small part in a typical science lesson. This has been verified by Lunzer and Gardner (3), who have analysed time spent reading in years 1 and 4 (see Chapter 1 for full lesson analysis).

In the first year, pupils spent 9% of their lesson reading.

In the fourth year, pupils spent 10% of their lesson reading.

They also found, most disturbingly, that this reading was done in extremely short bursts (3, p. 125):

	Duration			
	0–15 s	*16–30 s*	*31–45 s*	*45–60 s*
Year 1	75%	21%	3%	1%
Year 4	57%	36%	4%	3%

Over 90% of all pupils' reading was in bursts of under 30 seconds!

Further analysis showed what materials the pupils were reading (3, p. 123):

Reading	*Year 1*	*Year 4*
Textbook	30%	13%
Reference book	7%	1%
Library book	0%	1%
Exercise book	14%	43%
Blackboard	22%	25%
Other	27%	18%

Pupils reading their own exercise book or the blackboard for 10% of the lesson in bursts of under 30 seconds does not imply very much reading for understanding.

HMI in their *View of the Curriculum* (4, p. 25) say:

'Pupils need generally to increase their range and rate of comprehension which, in turn, requires an increasing commitment to sustained reading for which the school should make due provision.'

The emphasis on practical, independent work in the first two or three years in science has led to the use of large amounts of teacher-produced material and a real decline in the use of published material requiring sustained reading. Conversely, the low proportion of time spent reading text, reference, and library books in the fourth year means that there can be very little *independent* study by the pupils and again a decline in the use of any printed material, including class textbooks. Some science departments do not issue a textbook even to public examination candidates. According to the HMI survey it was because many departments found they could not afford them (5, p. 177) but the ASE found many teachers had stopped using textbooks because the pupils found them 'too difficult' (6). C.D. Gould in his study on the readability of school biology textbooks even goes so far as to draw the following conclusion:

'The results (of the study) confirmed that the texts presented serious problems of comprehension for some pupils. In the short term, classroom teachers should carefully consider the ways in which they use existing texts with their classes. The present shortage of textbooks in many of the schools may not, in fact, be such a serious problem—without them the pupils may be making more sense of their biology classes.' (7, pp. 248–52)

Budgets are being cut and prices raised, and many books commonly used have reading levels two years above the pupils in their target population.

The Effective Use of Reading project found science texts were amongst the most difficult, with first-year science standing out as particularly difficult. The marginally more difficult texts were used for homework (8, p. 2)!!

The difficulty for pupils reading a text for understanding can be assessed using various readability formulae (see later) which give the reading level of a text. The reading level of a text is a measure of how easily a piece of prose can be read with understanding. It is often quoted in terms of reading ages which are the average age at which pupils read that level of prose. Because the reading age is an average it does not follow that all pupils of that chronological age will be able to read the prose. Neither will pupils of different chronological ages but with the 'same' reading age have the same characteristics as readers. Readability, as gauged by reading levels, varies with: the reader's interest and speed; legibility of text; use of illustrations and colour; vocabulary; conceptual difficulty; syntax; and textual organization (9, p. 14).

There are many reasons why science texts are more difficult to read than those of English or history (most of these reasons will be discussed in the next section), and therefore the reading styles needed to interrogate scientific prose stand out as being very difficult for the pupil to acquire.

Lunzer and Gardner in *The Effective Use of Reading* have identified four reading styles:

Receptive—as in reading a story. This is the most familiar style.
Reflective—involves pauses for reflection. The reader will need to know when to pause, when to move back in the text, and also to retain motivation to continue.
Skimming—a very rapid read to establish what a text is about before deciding whether and where to read.
Scanning—a type of skimming but specially to find if a particular item is present in the text and to locate it (3, pp. 26-8).

Pupils on the whole have only been taught how to use the receptive style of reading, where the narrative carries them forward. Once a pupil has learnt to decode the words—and can now 'read'—very little attention is paid to teaching pupils the more advanced reading skills such as skimming, scanning, and the most difficult and important of all, reflective reading. It is these advanced reading skills that are most important for the successful interrogation of scientific prose.

This leads one to ask why the English department—traditionally regarded as the purveyor of reading skills—does not carry this burden for us so that we may preserve our precious, short lesson-time for teaching real science? One reason for the inability of many English departments to help other subjects develop reading skills is their preoccupation with fiction and narrative prose. The reading skills and motivational requirements of the non-narrative prose found in science texts are different and more demanding than those skills needed to read stories and the vivid descriptions found in passages used in English lessons.

Reading is as much a scientific activity as any other, including experimentation. Working scientists read journals alone for about five hours a week (10, p. 66). If we wish to give our pupils a taste of being a real scientist then reading should play an important part in our science lessons. The discovery of the neutron, positron, and deuteron in the 1930s is one of many examples of how scientists working in different countries but reading the same journals could work together using each others ideas and experimental findings (11). There is also the much broader need to make science accessible to all our pupils and not just the future scientists. In this country at the moment science is, par excellence, the subject reserved for experts. Many, even ostensibly well-educated people, ostentatiously deny they know any science at all. (How often have we as science teachers been infuriated by the remark, 'You teach science! Ah how clever!'.) If pupils can read about science it makes it potentially more accessible both in terms of present understanding and, even more important, of future interest. Most learning, after the exposition of school and lecture hall is over, is via books. If adults are alarmed by any scientific literature because of vividly remembered difficulties, then a major part of our society and its decision-making will be closed to them. It is also unrealistic for a teacher to imagine that within his or her well-structured, carefully prepared science lesson all will be understood by and available to the very brightest, the idiosyncratic, and the slowest pupil. If pupils can read with confidence and enthusiasm then an impossibly great weight of preparation is removed from the teacher, she/he may direct the pupils' attention to a book or the library without worrying if the pictures are sufficiently exciting or the librarian is free to do the explaining. Pupils come to an understanding of concepts in different ways; they may not understand the implications of the practical or the teacher's explanation (or hurried mumbled answer!). The opportunity to spend time mulling over a section in a book could give the pupil the extended answer to their question that would help them reach understanding.

The teaching of reflective scientific reading should be done within the context of the science lesson; the materials are at hand, it is a clearly needed skill, and only science teachers can use the teaching of this skill to improve their pupils' scientific understanding.

The Bullock committee's recommendation 88 points out that *all* teachers have a responsibility for teaching language skills:

'The extension of reading skills in and through normal activities is likely to be more effective than separately timetabled specialist reading periods.' (12, p. 522)

Reading is more important as a scientific technique than many practical skills. It is clear from the aims of science education given in Chapter 2 that they cannot be achieved without advanced reading skills.

Problems

It is only very recently that the special problems of reading in science have been explored. The Schools Council project *Reading for Learning in the Secondary School* has said that

'For most pupils, reading in science is probably one of the most challenging demands made on them throughout their secondary schooling. The reasons why reading in science is so difficult must begin with the difficulty of the language of science itself.' (8)

1 *The language of science*

Scientific language strives to be *precise*. Often this means that the reader is exposed to a large number of scientific terms, each with their own precise meaning outside familiar context clues, all embedded in an extremely complicated sentence structure.

(a) Vocabulary

The vocabulary of science is a great reading hurdle that science teachers have long recognized and tried to overcome. Many techniques have been used—underlining, special word lists, tests, and yet many laboratories do not have simple science and ordinary dictionaries. Not only do scientific terms have very precise meanings that embody large and complex concepts which the pupil may not fully grasp or feel confident in using, but they are often polysyllabic, difficult to spell, and to pronounce (for example, orthorhombic, phosphorus, diaphragm).

Another major problem lies not with the novelty of scientific words but the ordinary everyday words that have special meanings in science which repeatedly confuse pupils. In chemistry, for example, it is very difficult to get across the distinction between 'salt'—white stuff sprinkled on chips, 'salt'—a common name for sodium chloride, $NaCl$, and 'salt'—a compound where the H^+ of an acid has been replaced by a metal. 'Base', 'work', 'energy', 'power', 'stress', all have meanings in science that are totally different from their familiar meanings. (J.K. Gilbert (13) in his interviews with pupils has explored this overlap of everyday meaning with physicists' terms.

In a desire to be precise, many qualifying words and phrases are used: 'most', 'some', 'a few', etc., which make the reader hesitate—they need to evaluate the strength of the qualification. This puts a barrier between the reader and the information.

(b) Sentence structure

The structure of sentences in science is more complex than in many other forms of writing. Twenty-one words would be an average sentence length in a science text, yet in ordinary writing the average is only eleven words (6, p. 131). The increase in length means that there is usually more than one clause and the introduction of subordinate clauses is generally associated with an increase in the difficulty of a text. Even apparently simple sentences can pose problems to the unskilled reader.

'Sodium, which is metal belonging to Group 1 of the Periodic Table, is very reactive', is a seemingly very straightforward sentence but requires considerable reading skill. It is necessary to read, then scan forwards and backwards in order to pick out the subject and the verb and finally, to juggle the sentence round to extract its meaning (6, p. 131).'

Many other sentences involve complex clauses separated and linked by other words such as 'then', 'although', 'because', 'as', that demonstrate the relationship between the clauses. For example: 'If the element conducts electricity then it is likely to be a metal'. The classic example of this is the common multiple-choice question where there is an implied 'because' between the two parts of the question:

First Statement
An exothermic reaction gives out heat energy to the surroundings.

The products of an exothermic reaction possess less total energy than the reactants at the same temperature (14).

These exam questions are particularly hard for pupils to answer even though the word 'because' is familiar. Link words such as 'therefore', 'although', and 'until' are much harder as they have meanings that are difficult to define and are not very frequent in everyday speech. Without knowing these words the meaning of the sentence is lost.

(c) Types and forms of verbs

In scientific texts pupils will be exposed to a wide variety of forms of verbs, many of which will not be familiar and may make comprehension harder. Colin Harrison outlines these difficulties in *Readability in the Classroom*.

Formal accounts of experiments are largely written in the passive voice (rather than the much more accessible 'I' or 'we').

Active versus passive verb

Active verbs are easier to read and to recall than passive verbs, and they are less likely to be misunderstood when a negative statement is made.

For example, *The chairs were taken by the boys*
is harder than *The boys took the chairs.*
Similarly, *The pay-slips were not printed by the computer*
is harder than *The computer did not print the pay-slips.* (9, p. 23)

Often instructions in science and especially the 'laws' of science are written using nominalizations rather than active tenses of verbs.

Nominalization versus active verb

Active verbs are easier to comprehend and to recall than an abstract noun from the verb.

For example, *The reduction in the length of the string will produce an increase in the speed of the pendulum*
is harder than *If you reduce the length of the string you will increase the speed of the pendulum.* (9, p. 23)

Modal verbs

Generally speaking, modal verbs such as *might, could, may,* and *should* cause comprehension difficulties for poor readers, and make recall more difficult for fluent readers (9, p. 23).

There is also confusion over the use of the present continuous;
The liquid is boiling and the water is evaporating
and the present simple;
The liquid boils and the water evaporates.
Both can be used to describe what is happening but only the present simple can be used for apparatus, ideas, and for things that are universally true. There is a great difference implied in the two phrases, *It is burning*, and *It burns*. Then there is the present perfect that shows that something has been completed; *The water has evaporated.*

Compared to the prose with which pupils are most familiar, narrative prose, the variety of tenses and the precise implications of these tenses and forms can be very confusing.

(d) Lack of motivating factors

Much writing in science does not encourage children to start or to continue reading because it is without a narrative, which is a great incentive to continue reading. It is very impersonal in style with few human, social, or emotional tones—even asides on the life-histories of great scientists often make them appear extraordinarily dull.

Neither does writing in science have a very strong connection with the everyday life of pupils. Efforts are made by a few authors to overcome this difficult aspect but it is rarely successful. It has been said by Lunzer and Gardner that a difference in reading comprehension is a difference in willingness and ability to reflect on what is being read (3, p. 300). The impersonal style of scientific writing means there must be a *willingness to read* in the mind of the reader. It is clear that because of the very nature of scientific writing pupils are going to experience severe difficulties in their attempts to read science. It is also clear that writing in science cannot be simplified beyond the level of precision required. Technical terms and difficult concepts are intrinsic to science. Therefore, strategies for improving the pupils' reading skills to cope with these problems and especially that of reflective reading, are vitally important.

(e) Measuring the level of language difficulty

The difficulty the language of science poses for the reader can be crudely estimated by finding the reading level of a text. The reading level of a text can be found using one of the various readability formulae. These usually, however, only take into account word and sentence lengths.

Summary of research data on nine readability measures, and ratings of ease of application, from *Readability in the classroom*, Harrison 1980.

	Validity	Age level accuracy (8–16 age-range)	Ease of application
Flesch formula (Grade score)	●●●●	●●●	●●
Fry graph	●●●●	●●●	●●●
Powers–Sumner–Kearl formula	●●●●	●	●●●
Mugford formula and chart	●●●●	●●●●	●●
FOG formula	●●●	●●	●●●●
SMOG formula	●●●	●●	●●●●●
Dale–Chall formula	●●●●●	●●●●	●
Spache formula	●●●●	●●	●●
FORCAST formula	●●	●●	●●●●

Key: the more blobs the better   © COLIN HARRISON 1980

(Validity is usually assessed as the correlation between the reading level as found by the formula as against the level found by the pooled results of a group of teachers.)

In general, reading levels give a useful indication of the difficulty of a text but need to be used with the following cautionary notes in mind:

A readability score is only useful if the measure is a valid one and if the prose is suitable for analysis.

A reading level score is only accurate if the formula is a reliable one and the counts of linguistic features have been made accurately on an adequate text sample.

A readability score gives only an approximate indication of difficulty, accurate to about plus-or-minus one year.

Generally speaking, it is reasonable to assume that children can cope with texts up to two years above their own reading level provided that either the teacher's close support is available, or the child's motivation is high.

Never use a formula score to deny children access to what they want to read, but rather use a high score as a warning of potential difficulties ahead and the need for increased vigilance. (9 pp. 109–10)

Of course, when assessing the appropriateness of a text for a class one must also investigate the reading ability of the pupils themselves. Blanket testing—often an entry to the secondary school—gives us no more than a very inaccurate guide. There are various ways of telling if a pupil can cope with a text—but this will only refer to that particular text and pupil. The pupil can be assessed on various comprehension tests, their opinion as to the difficulty can be asked (this can be well done by asking pupils to underline hard passages in red, easy passages in blue, and scoring 0 (blue), 1 (no underlining), 2 (red)—the higher the score the more the difficulty), or by doing cloze exercises.

Methods for working out readability formulae and of carrying out cloze procedures are described later in this chapter.

2 The choice of books and materials

One major problem in choosing books and materials arises from the language difficulties inherent in scientific writing, which means that many science books and materials do not have a reading level or language style appropriate to the needs of pupils. Some efforts are being made by publishers, and some books and courses have made great efforts to keep the readability level suitably low. (The *Insight In Science* course (15) has a reading age of nine years for its core cards and for its extension work.)

Publishers are to some extent reluctant to publicize the reading levels of their books as they have a genuine fear that this data might be used by many teachers as too-accurate an indication of reading level, rather than as a general indication.

(a) Use of worksheets and back-up booklets

The increase in mixed-ability classes has made the choice of one class textbook extremely difficult, if not impossible, although a textbook could be a valuable resource. In such a situation there is often an unhappy compromise (2) between worksheets for the practical and question-answering part of the lesson and a miscellaneous collection of back-up booklets. The majority of pupils have a diet of worksheets and only the faster pupils are directed towards books when all the worksheet tasks have been done. Back-up materials for these courses are not very easy to find and are not usually linked to the course in any planned way. They are therefore not always suitable in terms of content or of level. Backup booklets/books for optional topics in the fourth and fifth years are even more difficult to find. The growth of worksheet-based courses continues, but many do not produce any material for extended reading or extension and some do not even produce a bibliography of useful books.

Mixed-ability groups in the fourth and fifth year are not uncommon where option systems and pupil choice do not allow separate groups, and when some teachers prefer to teach all abilities together. Buying one textbook that covers both a range of abilities of pupils and also different exam targets can pose severe problems—there are few single volumes that have such wide potential use.

(b) Expense

The HMI found that lack of money to buy books was given as the main reason for their absence in many schools (5, p. 177). Many textbooks are now available in paperback. This decreases their initial cost but means they have to be rapidly replaced. With the increase in numbers of science subjects offered in the fourth and fifth year—many of which are based on options, such as *Science at Work* (16), *Nuffield 13 to 16* (17) etc., the number of backup books needed is greatly increased. The variety of books with different levels and content required to provide a comprehensive science library is now enormous and vastly expensive.

(c) Book selection

A further problem resulting from the immense variety and range of books is the need for skill and time on the part of the teacher to read and assess books before buying them. The Bullock Committee recommended that:

> 'If a teacher is to plan individual instruction to meet specific needs, her first task is to assess the attainment level of every child and provide each with teaching material of the right level of readability'.   (12, 17.19)

However, it is hardly realistic to expect a teacher to do reading level surveys on all the books she/he buys—indeed it is only really practicable for the major outlays such as class texts where large, irrevocable sums of money and years of pupil time are involved.

In a comprehensive survey of teachers' methods of selecting books Kate Vincent found that:

> 'Few teachers were aware of the difficulties of skilful book selection or adopted a methodical approach to the problem, so that their choice of sources (of information about books) was often a haphazard or arbitary one.' (18, p. 155)

Information on books is available from many sources; catalogues, reps, inspection copies, reviews, libraries, exhibitions, colleagues, etc., but again for the busy practising teacher, or Head of Department, time to collect and process this information is very hard to find.

3 *Examinations*

In any survey of problems within a science department, the public examinations and their syllabuses will have a gloomy role to play. The exam-packing of the later years in secondary school and the consequent decrease in reading has been graphically described by HMI.

> 'Many pupils were developing attitudes to reading which undermined the good work done in primary and early secondary years and might well outlast the examinations themselves.' (5, p. 74)

The decline in use of the textbook or reference book in science lessons from first to fourth year is probably largely due to the pressure of the examinations.

The problems facing pupils and their teachers in science are inherent in scientific writing with its complex vocabulary, sentence structure, use of tenses, and lack of external motivating factors. These problems can only be overcome by teaching our students advanced reading skills such as reflective reading so that they can cope with these difficulties, and also by providing pupils with plenty of stimulating books to read that are at an appropriate level.

Strategies

The benefits to the science lesson of using reading activities

As was said at the beginning of this chapter, there are many reasons why it should be the science teacher who teaches pupils the skills needed to read science texts. In many ways this aspect of science teaching will not only help the pupils to understand science concepts more easily but will have other useful spin-offs in the laboratory, in class management, and in broadening the relationship between teacher and pupil.

Practical work needs to be prepared for in advance and interpreted when completed. There are many ways of doing this—the class-questioning/hypothesizing beforehand, and the class discussion afterwards are both very common. However, in mixed ability classes the opportunities for class discussion are more difficult to fit in, as pupils are largely working at their own pace. Consequently class discussions must be planned at the beginning and only about topics, rather than after individual experiments. Pupils need to be stimulated to think about what they are going to do and what they have seen. Reading is one of the best ways of matching their practical work to theory. It is also excellent real scientific practice to read about one's experiment and see whether the results are as expected, match others' results, and to see if theory provides a sufficient explanation.

Pupils in most science classes and especially if mixed ability will never finish their experiments simultaneously and often there is an uncomfortable gap between the finishing of the practical and the end of the lesson. It is often not possible to draw the class together for a discussion, start a new section or practical, and the teacher may still be occupied with the experimenters. This hiatus provides an excellent opportunity to do some reading or a reading-skills activity that is related to the practical work newly completed. It also provides a calming influence in a laboratory, where many different practicals are going on simultaneously—straining the nerves of teachers and technicians.

The following sections consider some points to think about when choosing books or materials, how to improve reading skills in the laboratory, and finally how a textbook might be used.

1 *Choosing books and materials*

(a) What to look for

When buying reading materials three major factors should be investigated and appear to be right for the target pupils, assuming all potential material covers the right content. They are:

(i) attractiveness   (ii) clarity   (iii) level.

Attractiveness is not very difficult to assess; if a book has interesting subject matter, good pictures and diagrams, and is well-designed it will appeal to pupils initially (as well as to their teachers). One can, however, have too much of a good thing. In one modern chemistry textbook there were no less than eight or nine pictures and diagrams per page (mostly in colour) and a double-columned text that was so broken up by the distractingly eye-catching pictures it became very difficult to follow.

Clarity in a text is much more difficult to assess and involves personal judgements and preferences. The structure of a book—as shown by its contents page—gives the best idea of how the author sees his/her subject. If this is incompatible with one's own view then pupils are likely to suffer some confusion between the two different approaches. (I, for example, like information about elements in chemistry books to be arranged in groups as in the Periodic Table. I would not find books with chapters on metals dealing with all metals from sodium to copper very helpful.) If one is comparing several books on the same topic it is a good idea to have a particular idea or concept that will (or should) appear in all of them and see which explanation appears to be the easiest and best for the pupils to understand. Layout, the use of spaces, headings and subheadings, underlining and use of colour can all aid clarity so that the important is easily identified. The use of different typography—italics, capital letters, and bold type—can emphasize new words and concepts in a helpful way. Summaries often reinforce the connections and the importance of concepts. Diagrams can be a very clear way of presenting information, as can graphs and pictures. Sometimes practical instructions within a textbook that is mainly theoretical prose can detract from the clarity by interrupting the continuity.

Is the book the right level for the pupil? The level of a book is intimately connected to the match between the pupil's reading age and the book's readability score. The readability score of the book should be roughly the same as the reading age of the pupil if it is to be read in class. Books that are to be read without the teachers' support (and this might include backup materials to be used within a class or library as well as homework) should be two years below the pupils' reading age.

B. Prestt in the ASE's *Language in Science* has warned teachers of too blind a reliance on readability scores. She says:

'Readability and understandability are not the same thing. A low readability score is likely to equate with familiar words and simple sentences and this in turn is likely to be associated with an easy to understand presentation of content. But this relationship is not inevitable, so that again the teacher's judgement is of the utmost importance.' (6, p. 125)

The readability score of a book is usually assessed on average sentence length and number of syllables per word. There are many methods of assessing readability, all of which are clearly outlined in C. Harrison *Readability in the Classroom* (9). Three simple-to-use methods are given here.

(b) How to use a readability formula and a cloze procedure
Of the readability formulae discussed in *Readability in the Classroom* the Dale–Chall formula appears to be the best but is almost impossibly time-consuming for a working teacher (9, p. 74–7).

Two other methods provide valid and reliable results and are quite easy to operate. It is important before beginning to establish various definitions.

(i) *A word* is a string of letters or characters delimited by spaces. Therefore hyphenated words, numbers such as 15.9, 1964–5, and abbreviations such as M.Sc count as one word.

(ii) *Syllables*—each vowel sounded in a word corresponds to one syllable. So in the words *Jan, met, Jim, for, but,* and *cry* each vowel (a, e, i, o, u, y) corresponds to a single syllable. Longer words such as straight, write, which, splice, or boot still only count as one syllable, since there is only one vowel sound in each (ay, eye, i, eye, oo). Words ending in -ed may look as if they should have more than one syllable, but this is rarely the case. Think of combed, guessed, or grouped. In each there is still only one vowel sound. Two sorts of word will present problems, and these are ambiguous cases and abbreviations. For example, is piano three syllables or two? Is visual three syllables or two? Is iron one syllable or two? There are no fixed answers to these questions, since pronounciation will vary according to differences in accent (9, p. 65).

(iii) *Sentences*—it is, strictly speaking, preferable that the samples should all be of equal length, otherwise the samples will contribute unequally to the final score. We cannot therefore simply work from the end of the sentence which is running at word 100, at least not directly. The solution is to consider the part of the sentence up to word 100 as a fraction of its total length, and then to add this to the number of complete sentences. Thus if in a sample text, there are six complete sentences before the oblique stroke, followed by nine words of a 30-word sentence, the total number of sentences per hundred words is therefore 5 16/20, and if we divide this figure into 100 we obtain the average number of words per sentence.

(iv) *Accuracy in calculation*—when calculating the formulae, work to three decimal places throughout. Round the final result to one decimal place (9, p. 66–7).

Three samples taken from different sections of the text must be used.

The Flesch Formula

1 Count the average number of words per sentence.

2 Count the average number of syllables per 100 words.

3 Using a ruler, see where the line joining the words per sentence and the syllables per 100 words bisects the centre.

Syllables per 100 words

Reading ease score

Words per sentence

Very easy

Easy

Fairly easy

Standard

Fairly difficult

Difficult

Very difficult

© RUDOLF FLESCH

The Fry Graph

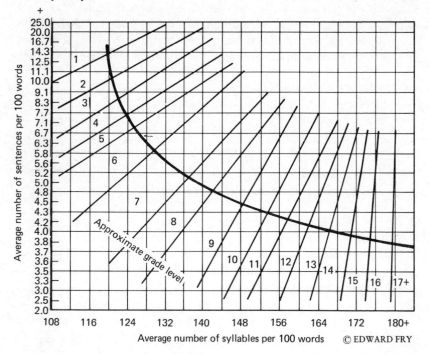

Average number of syllables per 100 words   © EDWARD FRY

This is one of the most straightforward ways of obtaining a readability index. The graphical form is helpful for a number of reasons: it saves time on making calculations; it offers visual information when numerical results might give a spurious impression of accuracy; the user of the graph can tell at a glance if a passage is in comparative terms more difficult than average in vocabulary or in sentence length. This final point is not generally realized, but clearly if the curve represents normal texts, points above the line, or towards the top right quadrant, will represent passages with higher than average vocabulary difficulty, while points below the curve, towards the bottom left quadrant, will suggest greater than average sentence length. These are the directions for using the readability graph:

- Randomly select three sample passages and count out exactly 100 words each, beginning with the beginning of a sentence.
- Count the number of sentences in the 100 words, calculating the length of the fraction of the last sentence to the nearest one-tenth.
- Count the total number of syllables in the 100-word passage. If you don't have a hand counter available, an easy way is to simply put a mark above every syllable over one in each word, then when you get to the end of the passage, count the number of marks and add 100.
- Enter the graph with the average numbers of sentences and syllables; plot a dot where the two lines intersect. The area where the dot is plotted will give you the approximate US grade level. The UK reading level is 5 + US grade.
- If a great deal of variability is found in syllable count or sentence count, putting more samples into the average is desirable.
- When counting syllables for numerals and abbreviations, count one syllable for each symbol. For example, *1945* is four syllables, *IRA* is three syllables, and *&* is one syllable (9, pp. 73–4).

The one I find convenient to use is the McLaughlin's Smog Grading although it is not as valid as the other two methods.

1 Select three passages of ten sentences from the beginning, middle, and end of the text.
2 Count every word of three or more syllables in these sentences.
3 Find the square root.
4 Add eight. This is the reading age in years.

These formulae give the reading level of a text, if a teacher wishes to find out whether a book matches her pupils' reading ages. The teacher can also carry out a Cloze procedure test. Here a passage is selected from a text and words omitted regularly, e.g. every fifth or sixth word. The pupil then has to read the passage and fit in the correct word (that is, any word that makes complete sense). 60% success means the pupil could use the material independently; 40–50% with teacher support; below 40% is described as the 'frustration level'. This is a useful technique as it actually matches pupil and text.

A *cloze procedure*

Energy and living things

We started our work on energy _____ talking about ourselves—how we all _____ energy to live. When you think _____ all the movements we carry out _____ in and day out, you will _____ that we must have energy for _____. Even when you are asleep parts _____ your body are in motion all _____ time. You continue to breathe, and _____ you breathe your lungs become inflated _____ deflated several times a minute. To _____ this your rib-cage has to expand _____ contract. Your heart is moving all the _____ pumping blood round your body. So _____ if you did not walk or _____ or wave your arms about or _____, you would still require energy.

In _____ form do we take in energy? _____ where do we get this supply _____ energy?

If you think of the different _____ of food you eat, you will _____ discover that it all comes from _____. Bread, potatoes, fruit—all come from _____. What about meat, you will say? _____ eat plants for their food. If _____ think about this for a little _____ making a list of all the _____ you had for your meals, say, _____, and noting where they come from, _____ will see that plants provide us _____ all our food, and so with _____ our energy. How important is the _____ work! Without him there would be _____ to work the machines which are _____ an important part of our modern _____. We could perfectly well do without _____—although our life would be much _____ difficult and uninteresting—but we could _____ do without plants and animals, for _____ them we should die.

Plants, of _____, cannot grow without sunlight—and so_____ come back to what we said _____ first, that the Sun is the _____ of all our energy.

From *Science for the 70's, Book One* (19, pp. 46-7)

Even if there is a match of reading levels and scores, the teacher must also judge texts for other aspects that might cause problems. Vocabulary is partly taken care of in the reading ability assessment, but the quantity of new technical terms introduced to pupils may be too high or too low for the pupils' level. (The level does not always need to be low—for examination texts the level will be that of the final examination or even slightly higher.) A text that has very low redundancy, (a high density of concepts) may prove indigestible—it is very difficult for even motivated, skilful adults to read a passage where every phrase counts. The subject matter and the concepts involved may be too demanding or not sufficiently demanding. Sentence complexity is taken into account in readability assessments only in terms of length. Yet it is probably one of the hardest things for science teachers to judge, as we are so used to moving backwards and forwards within sentences, and so much of the text's content is so well-known we often understand without reading. The English department might be very helpful here.

Recommendation three of the National Book League's *Books for Schools* is that:

'Methods of book selection, *readability* levels, ... should form an essential part of initial and in-service training. As book selection is particularly a part of the responsibility of teachers in middle management the inclusion of this work in in-service courses is of particular importance.'   (20)

(c) Textbooks

Choosing a class textbook has its own special considerations in addition to the above, not least because such large amounts of money are involved. Here it is vitally important to determine how the textbook is going to be used. For example:

  (i) as practical instructions
 (ii) as an explanatory text
(iii) as a summary of information
 (iv) as an expansion of information into links with industry and manufacturing processes
  (v) for providing questions either for homework or as typical exam questions
 (vi) providing exercises
(vii) as a reference book
(viii) as revision notes.

Clearly the textbook should meet most of your requirements.

The clarity of explanation of a 'test' concept or idea is clearly very important. Indexes should be tested for adequacy—again the 'test' concept or idea could be looked up in the index to see how many and how useful the references are. (Indexes are remarkably important and much neglected. If pupils can use an index and the teacher expects them to use it and the index then proves inadequate, it is very discouraging.) The readability score is important—if the book is to be used frequently for homework it will have to be considerably lower than if the book is only to be used in class.

As textbooks used for an examination have to be at the level of the examination it means that it is even more vital, if pupils are to work at home as they must, that the pupils have the necessary skills to reach independent reading levels using that text.

When the textbook is being chosen for a particular examination course it is extremely difficult for inexperienced teachers to judge whether the level and emphasis of the book is appropriate. Examination syllabuses and examination questions change over the years, as do textbooks, and it is difficult to ensure a match between the two. Very valuable and interesting discussions on the theme of 'my favourite textbook for course X' between different experienced teachers can be an easy and pleasant way of establishing a pecking order of books. (In London the C^3G Chemistry group had a fascinating discussion on books for O and A level chemistry which evolved into a list of books starred for appropriateness.) If teachers bring to their discussions a selection of textbooks, this also helps overcome the difficulty of never seeing the books together so that they may be compared.

(d) Collecting information and comparing books

There is no shortage of information on books and indeed teachers are 'often bewildered by the array of information sources at their disposal' (18, p. 155). The Lady David *Committee of Inquiry into School Book Supply* found that the inability to compare books was a major drawback to teachers choosing books sensibly (21, p. 65). Clearly teachers have not got the time to look thoroughly at all the possible books and so a first selection has to be made from catalogues, reviews, colleagues' recommendations, and book displays at teachers' centres or conferences. 'The main sources of information on books for teachers are the publishers' catalogues. Unfortunately many of these are beautiful to look at but difficult and confusing to use'(18, p. 158). The National Book League has made a recommendation to the publishers that, if followed, would make catalogues much more helpful to teachers (19, p. 30). All science departments should have an up-to-date full collection of catalogues, stored centrally in the department for easy access by teachers.

Permanent displays of books in teachers' centres or provided by the LEA are extremely helpful and would be even more useful if time could be allowed by the schools for teachers to visit them. The ASE conference, which is held every year, provides an unparalled opportunity to see the whole range of science books available. The Educational Publishers Council has a major exhibition of school books that visits most large regional centres every two years and they will also arrange with publishers to send relevant books to teachers' courses and conferences. Their address is Education

Publishers Council, 19 Bedford Square, London WC1 3HJ. Reviews, especially those in the *School Science Review* and *TES*, are helpful but no substitute for seeing the book itself.

Once a shortlist of possibilities has been established, inspection copies can be requested so that the relative virtues of each book can be studied by the teacher and by the other members of the department. The books should be circulated round the members of the department with a form for comments. (This is extremely valuable in-service training for young or jaded teachers as it makes them think about their teaching and the subject.) Background books and booklets have very different functions and are mainly to provide a stimulating and interesting read. Here the attractiveness to the eye and the imagination are very important but should not be so overwhelming that the appeal of the pictures detracts from the interest of the text. These books are best bought singly initially and then their popularity monitored by either the science teacher or the librarian. It is not so vital to assess each book for level, clarity, etc. beforehand as the outlay is less and the errors can be balanced out later. If a book is popular more copies can be bought.

A collection of background books/materials that is relevant to the part of the course being studied at the moment should be available on display in the laboratory. It is nice to make a fuss about a new book. The pupils know it is there; you, the teacher, are pleased to have it; so the feeling that books matter is encouraged. The display should be near the back of the laboratory away from the main practical area (as much as possible), so when pupils are directed to the reading/book area they are in a slightly quieter and less buffeted space. Displays of books on topics and new books in science should be arranged with the librarian in the school library.

There is something to be said for leaving the traditional educational publishers and looking round local bookshops to see what they offer (and know will sell) to children. Often teachers prefer rather conservative, scientifically-written books that are like those they had at school. They will write and then buy books that pupils may find rather dull. The general publisher and local bookseller have a different approach and are geared to selling straight to the pupil consumer and not to teachers, which makes pupil-taste a much more powerful force on the publisher. Many of these books are just as respectable but more appealing; one has only to look at the Hamlyn and Ladybird series to see how successful popular books on science can be. Topical newspaper cuttings and articles on science also generate much enthusiasm and provide links with the news and everyday happenings. These cuttings should be displayed briefly or put into a plastic folder and pointed out to pupils; then after 1–2 weeks filed or thrown away. There are few things more calculated to put pupils off reading than yellowed, faded, torn newsprint pinned to a science noticeboard for years. Science or hobby-based periodicals can be displayed and then stored in the science laboratory after being removed from the library. Again these should have a brief public life and not lie around. The pupils should be encouraged to read the scientific magazines, such as *New Scientist* and *Scientific American*, both of which should be available in all school libraries. Examples of real scientific articles, from *Nature* or more specialized journals, should be available either in the library or department for pupils to look at and to read. All pupils who learn science should have seen these articles, even if the language and content is far above them!

Pupils are most frequently required to read worksheets. Here the work required from the pupil is as vital as the attractiveness, clarity, and level of the sheet. Most of the points on worksheets are covered in Chapter 5.

(e) Administration within the department

If a department has large numbers of books, booklets, pamphlets, worksheets, cuttings, and periodicals it will need to catalogue them so that all teachers (and pupils when necessary) are aware of these resources and where they can be found. (Other departments might also find these materials useful and should be encouraged to browse.)

How and where books and written resources are stored depends very largely on the arrangement of the laboratories but if laboratories are subject-based it makes sense to have all materials related to that subject on shelves or filed in the labs. It is important to have books (even those that are not on display or in a current collection in a reading area) to be very visible so pupils associate science with attractive books and reading. Cuttings and other printed material should be indexed and filed. There should be a central catalogue in the science department and the library of all these materials should be on the same pattern as that used by the library.

2 *Reading for understanding*

'A curriculum should provide for the continuous development of skill in reading throughout the years of schooling, from the recognition of words to the comprehension of complicated materials.'   (4, p. 24)

(a) Reflective reading—DARTS

Roy Fawcett, in a study undertaken for the Schools Council project, *The Effective Use of Reading*, came to the firm conclusion that skill-based, highly structured courses improved the reading skills of pupils:

'We conclude: The evidence clearly indicates that children of 10, 11, 12 and 15 years of age benefitted at a highly significant level in developing speed and accuracy of reading, wider vocabularies and greater understanding of what they read from the use of SRA laboratories.' (3, p. 227)

('SRA laboratories' are a highly structured means of developing competency in literacy and reading comprehension. There is a full description in *The Effective Use of Reading* (3).)

The Effective Use of Learning project has been followed up by the Reading and Learning in the Secondary School project which has, in print, *Reading for Learning in the Sciences* (8), in which the techniques for improving pupils' general reading skills have been applied to reading in science. This has resulted in the production of various *'Directed Activities Related to Texts'* (DARTS). DARTS are designed to direct and focus the pupils' attention on the text, so that they can pick out the important parts of a text and learn to read reflectively (8).

There are two main types of DARTS:

(A) *Reconstruction or completion-directed reading activities*;
(B) *Analysis of target-directed reading activities.*

These two types of DARTS involve different activities—they are shown in the table overleaf.

Here are some descriptions of the simpler DARTS with examples; a much fuller description with more examples is to be found in *Reading for Learning in the Sciences* (8).

(A) *Reconstruction* DARTS

1 *Text completion* (i) Prediction of words deleted on irregular basis Here the teacher can delete words that she/he feels will demand thought about the science concepts involved. The information in the rest of the text is used to provide scientific context clues to

DARTS Classification of Directed Activities Related to Text

RECONSTRUCTION DARTS
(use modified text?)
*Pupil task—Completion
                activities with
                deleted text*
1 **Text completion**
   (i) Pupil prediction of
       deleted *words*.
   (ii) Pupil prediction of
        deleted *phrases, clauses
        or sentences*.
   (iii) Pupil prediction of *labels*
         of parts of text where
         these are deleted.
2 **Diagram completion**
   Pupil prediction of deleted
   labels and/or *parts of
   diagrams* using text and
   diagrams as sources of
   information. (See
   Diagrammatic
   representation.)
3 **Table completion**
   Completion *of tables* with
   words or *phrases deleted*
   using table categories and
   text as sources of reference.
4 **Completion activities with
   disordered text**
   (i) Predicting logical *order* or
       time sequence of segments
       of text.
   (ii) *Classifying segments*
        according to categories
        given by teacher.
5 **Prediction**
   Pupil *prediction of next
   part(s)* of text with segments
   presented in sequence.

ANALYSIS DARTS (Use straight
text)
*Pupil task—Text marking and
                labelling*
1 **Underlining**
   Search for specified targets in
   text which relate to *one*
   aspect of the content.
2 **Labelling**
   Pupil labelling of segments of
   text (e.g. paragraphs) which
   deal with *different* aspects of
   text with labels provided by
   teachers.
3 **Segmenting**
   (i) Segmenting of paragraphs
       or text into information
       units.
   (ii) Labelling of segments of
        text without labels
        provided by teacher;
        producing classification
        for segments of text.
Pupil task—recording
4 **Diagrammatic representation**
   Constructing diagrams of
   content of text making a
   choice from Flow diagrams,
   Hierarchies, Networks, or
   Models, Continua
5 **Tabular representation**
   Pupil construction of tables
   from information given in
   text.
6 **Questions**
   (i) Pupils study text to
       decide how questions
       would be answered.
   (ii) Pupils generate questions
        after studying text.
7 **Summary**
   Summary of information
   utilising headings and/or
   diagrammatic representation.

(8)

fill in the gaps. So a paragraph at the beginning and end of a passage is usually left complete to provide context and to encourage reflective thought. Texts must be chosen with care so that there are genuine clues and the concepts are not too mixed.

Sexual reproduction

Sexual reproduction involves the joining or fusing together of two cells. One of these reproductive cells comes from a male animal and the other comes from a female. The reproductive cells are called gametes. The fusing of two gametes is called fertilization and the resulting, composite cell is called a zygote. The most important aspect of fertilization is the fusion of the nuclei of the male and female gametes, because the factors which determine the characteristics of the individual that grows from the zygote are in these nuclei.

Fertilization, in short, is the fusion of the _____ of male and female _____ to form a _____ from which can develop a new _____ .

In animals, the male _____ are sperms, which are produced in the reproductive organs called testes. The female _____ is an ovum which is produced in a reproductive organ called an ovary.

Some animals such as earthworms and snails are hermaphrodite, that is, they have both testes and ovaries, but in most animals the sexes are separate.

Internal and external fertilization. In most fish and amphibia fertilization is external. The female lays the _____ first and the male _____ them by placing _____ on them afterwards. A behaviour pattern which brings the sexes into _____ usually ensures that sperm is shed near the eggs and so _____ the chances of fertilization.

In reptiles and birds, the eggs are _____ inside the body of the female by the male's pasing sperms into the egg ducts. A _____ meets the _____ and fertilizes it before it is laid. Very little development of the egg takes place before laying, however, and the embryo grows in the egg, after it has left its mother's body.

In mammals, _____ are placed in the body of the female and the _____ are fertilized internally. They are not laid after fertilization but _____ in the female's body while they develop to quite an advanced stage, after which the young are born more or less fully formed, being fed on _____ from the mammary glands and protected by their parents until they become independent.

From *An Introduction to Biology* (22)

2 *Table completion* Pupils are given a ready-made table and a prose passage. They have to fill in the table with information that is buried in the text. (In science, this is quite a common activity where the information lies in practical results and observations.)

Chemical properties of metals
Most metals, when they are placed in water, will not react at all, though iron will slowly rust and copper may turn slightly green. Sodium, however, will react violently with water, and potassium will catch fire. Calcium will react slightly less vigorously with water than sodium. In each of the above three reactions hydrogen gas is produced.

$$sodium + water \rightarrow sodium\ hydroxide + hydrogen$$

As sodium, potassium and calcium are so reactive, they must be stored away from water and air. They are usually kept in paraffin oil and locked away for safety. Mercury is very poisonous, both as a liquid and a vapour. It must therefore be kept in a locked poisons cupboard and used only in a fume cupboard by the teacher.

Most metals will react with dilute acids. Sodium and potassium will react explosively to produce a salt and hydrogen gas.

$$sodium + dilute\ hydrochloric\ acid \rightarrow sodium\ chloride + hydrogen$$

Zinc will react vigorously with dilute acids to produce a salt and hydrogen.

$$zinc + dilute\ hydrochloric\ acid \rightarrow zinc\ chloride + hydrogen$$

Iron reacts similarly to zinc. Copper, silver and gold do not react with dilute acids to yield hydrogen.

From *Chemistry* (23)

Chemical properties of metals			
Reaction	*Which metals react?*	*What are the products of the reaction?*	*Which metals do not react?*
1 With water			
2 With air			
3 With acids			

3 *Diagram completion* Pupils are given a text and an incomplete diagram. They must read the passage, then underline labels of parts and add them to the diagram. Pupils then add to the diagram the function of each part.

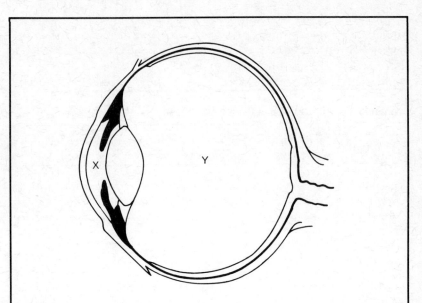

The eye
1. Underline the names of the parts of the eye, and mark in the passage any information that tells you where the parts are located.
2. Now finish labelling the diagram of the eye, deciding what the parts are like. If you are not sure about a part of the diagram draw an arrow to the bottom of the page. We will discuss the parts we are not sure about at the end of the lesson.

The eye
The eye is a spherical structure used for seeing. The eye is made of three layers that surround a sticky substance called the vitreous humour. The outermost layer is called the sclerotic layer. This is very tough and holds the eye in shape. The middle layer is called the choroid layer and contains blood vessels. The inner layer is the retina which contains two types of cells that are sensitive to light. The impulses from this layer are taken from the eye to the brain in the optic nerve. The lens of the eye is attached to the choroid layer by the suspensory ligaments. The lens is clear and helps focus light rays onto a very sensitive part of the retina at the back of the eye called the yellow spot. In front of the lens is the iris which can be many colours in people from blue to dark brown. The iris opens in dim light to allow light to enter the eye through the pupil. In very bright light the iris closes to stop too much light entering the eye through the pupil and damaging the retina. At the front of the eye the schlerotic layer becomes transparent to allow light into the eye. This is called the cornea.

4 *Sequencing* A text is cut up into segments of equal size. The pupil's task is to put the segments in an appropriate sequence. (Instruction for an experiment is the simplest example, but life cycles or processes, for example, could be used.)

This activity has often been used successfully by teachers to make sure that pupils know what they have to do during an experiment and to give pupils a sense of time and logical sequencing.

How long does it take to cook an egg?

If you have a boiled egg for breakfast, you probably prefer to have it cooked for a particular period of time, depending upon whether you want to have it hard or soft. Do you put your egg into boiling water or do you put it into cold water and heat it up from cold? When do you start timing the cooking process? Does it make any difference if the egg has been kept in a refrigerator? Do fresh eggs take a longer or a shorter time than others to cook?

In order to carry out an investigation into cooking time, you will need to decide on a method to judge when the egg is properly cooked. Many people do this by the hardness of the egg white. This will be a simple way to start this investigation.

Sort these sentences into the correct order for your experiment by cutting them up and sticking them in your book in order.

Cork the tubes and stand them in a rack.

Watch the egg white carefully and stop the clock when the egg white has set (you can judge when it is no longer possible to see through the tube, a mark with a Chinagraph pencil on the back of the tube will help).

Now take one of the tubes from the rack, remove the cork and clamp it in the beaker of water, at the same time start a stop-clock.

Record the time taken. How does the time taken compare with the time for which you like your egg cooked?

Place a beaker, half-full of water, on a tripod or an electric hot plate and clamp a thermometer ($-10°C$ to $110°C$) so that the bulb is in the water to the correct depth.

Heat the water to about $100°C$. Adjust the heat so that the temperature of the water is kept constant.

Use a teat pipette to transfer a suitable amount of egg white to a number of small test-tubes.

Crack an egg carefully and separate the egg white from the yolk.

From *Projects in Chemistry* (24)

B *Analysis* DARTS
These texts are to help the pupil focus on targets which have been decided previously by the teacher. Targets might include names of structures, functions of structures, evidence, etc.

1 *Underlining* The teacher reads a prose passage and identifies what she/he wishes the pupils to focus on as a target. The text is then given to the pupils who are told to read it through and then to underline, for example, the main idea and then sentences that give examples of this idea. This is illustrated on the page opposite.

This, of course, is the initial learning stage. It is necessary before pupils can make their own notes.

The texts used for DARTS should be directly relevant to the course, with different texts being used for different DARTS.

Teacher and pupils should discuss the purpose and usefulness of DARTS before the pupils begin to work with them. All pupils can be given copies of the text which they then work on and complete. After the DART has been discussed in small groups of two or three pupils, there should be a class discussion. The pupils can then keep the text in their files where it can be used for revision later in the course. Pupils can work individually or in groups of two or three pupils. The latter allows discussion and constructive argument but does not permit some pupils to become passive listeners as often happens in larger groups. Weak and fluent readers can work together or the teacher can read out the text with the class to ensure that all pupils understand the text. A class discussion after the pupils have completed the task brings ideas together and can be a productive and lively discussion where pupils' understanding of the concepts can be explored. These activities and those outlined in more detail in *Reading for Learning in the Sciences* (8) should help the pupil to learn to read receptively.

Two other reading styles are important in science: *skimming* and *scanning*. Pupils should be given help and encouragement to acquire these skills.

(b) Skimming
Skimming is used to find out quickly the contents of a long passage, chapter, or book. The reader must read quickly and selectively, focussing on the beginnings and summaries of each section or paragraph, skipping most of what is inessential.

Most comprehension exercises set to pupils are too short and too predictable to provide any real practice at skimming (see the

Chemical competitions
Underline the main idea in this passage and then, in a different colour, the different examples given of this idea.

Chemical competitions
Chemicals can enter into competitions with each other. Luckily for us chemical competition is generally simpler than human competition, because there are usually very few things that can alter the result. We can therefore often predict with great success what will happen in a chemical competition. A simple example of chemical is found when lead oxide and zinc are heated together. When the mixture is warmed a glow is observed. A chemical reaction—or competition—is taking place. When it is over, and the mixture has cooled, we are left with a white powder and globules of a grey metal. The white powder is zinc oxide, and the grey metal is lead. The reaction may be expressed in words:

$$\text{lead oxide} + \text{zinc} \rightarrow \text{zinc oxide} + \text{lead}$$

The two metals have been in competition for the oxygen, held at the beginning by the lead. Since the zinc has taken this oxygen and formed it into its own oxide, zinc is the winner. The lead is unable to recapture the oxygen, and zinc oxide must therefore be more stable than lead oxide. Chemists sometimes use the word affinity (meaning relationship, as in marriages) to describe what happens. They would say that zinc has a greater affinity for oxygen than lead has.

It is very useful to be able to predict how substances will behave when they compete for oxygen. For example, we can predict that, given enough heat, carbon will take oxygen away from iron ore (iron oxide). That is why, during iron manufacture, iron ore is heated with carbon (in the form of coke):

$$\begin{array}{c}\text{iron oxide} \\ \text{(iron ore)}\end{array} + \begin{array}{c}\text{carbon} \\ \text{(coke)}\end{array} \rightarrow \text{iron} + \text{carbon dioxide}$$

When the oxygen is removed from a substance the process is called reduction. Reduction of iron oxide by carbon will not take place until the mixture of oxide and carbon has been heated to a very high temperature. The reactants have a motive for the reaction because the oxide of carbon is more stable than that of iron, but a stimulus or preparation in the form of energy is needed, just as an athlete may want to do well in a race, but cannot do so until, by training and by control of his diet, his body is capable of the required performance. Athletes may still surprise us in the way they perform in a competition. Chemicals, on the other hand, have no choice in the way they react in a given situation.
(From the Revised Nuffield Chemistry Study Sheet, Competitions.) (25)

Jumblies passage in Chapter 5 *Worksheets*, p. 91). Usually readers have to be able to find their answers in any part of the text, to focus on one section for many answers and leave completely unread whole sections. This causes pupils very great difficulty and insecurity.

Before attempting to skim through a passage pupils should be aware of the importance of the *structure* of a text. Titles, subtitles, headings—all give clear clues as to the content hierarchy of the text. Within the text itself, most writers give introductions to a new section and usually summarize at the end. These may be actually headed 'Introduction' or 'Summary'. The typography—bold type, italics, capital letters—all emphasize the important. Illustrations and numbers often catch the eye. Connectives or signal words that indicate relationships between ideas *must* be thoroughly understood by pupils or the whole meaning of a passage will be lost.

Words such as 'because', 'since', 'if', 'unless', 'though', 'although' occur very frequently in science and their meaning is not nearly as easy to guess from the context as would be an unknown noun (26, p. 107–12). The art of skimming lies in the pupils' ability to quickly pick out the key sentences and words and to ignore the rest. Pupils can be given short passages and asked to underline the key sentences and cross out all anecdotes, examples, etc. This can be extended by giving the pupils much longer passages (of two or more pages) and a time limit (to prevent them reading continuously). Other long passages can be given and the pupils asked to write down the main ideas of each passage, again within a time limit. Pupils can also be given a variety of passages and asked which passage would help to answer different questions.

When pupils have learnt to skim extended passages and chapters of books, the skimming can be extended to whole books. Books provide many clues about their content in their blurb, preface, introduction, contents, index, author's name, date, and even the cover of the book itself. Pupils should learn to 'read' these clues (see Chapter 8, *Information skills*). Success in the skill of skimming would 'help avert the situation in which a child is halfway through copying or making notes on a passage before he realizes that it is not after all dealing with the issue he wanted to raise' (26).

(c) Scanning
Scanning is used to locate particular known items of information within a text. Passages with numbered paragraphs are given to the pupils with the instruction that they must find out which paragraph contains the information x—again within a time limit to prevent continuous reading.

Chapters and books can be given eventually and the pupil must write down the page or section where the information is located. It is important that pupils are given examples (and told that they will be given examples) that do NOT contain the information required; very often teachers carefully structure their work so there is assured success. Pupils then get very dismayed when the teacher asks them to do a project or large assignment and there is nothing in the first book that comes to hand.

Finally, one of the most important aids to reading is a *dictionary*. Each laboratory should have an easy-to-understand, modern dictionary so that pupils will automatically look up words in the dictionary for spellings and meanings rather than ask the teacher.

3 *Use of a textbook*

Textbooks represent such a great financial investment and (if well chosen) such a rich resource that they should not be left on shelves or in lockers. Teachers often say that textbooks are too difficult for pupils to use but if pupils have been trained in advanced reading skills, many of these difficulties will have been overcome. Apart from giving training in advanced reading skills there are other things a teacher can do to help his/her pupils use textbooks successfully.

Textbooks are sometimes given to the pupils to be kept at home while another book or a selection of textbooks are used in school. This may prevent loss in transit or the book being forgotten but it also means the pupil has to familiarize him/herself with the textbook without the help of the teacher. It is a good idea to use the same book in class and at home for at least some of the time, so that the pupil becomes used to its structure, terminology, style, index, and so on. We all know how we become accustomed to certain books and even in later years many teachers have a much-thumbed copy of some ancient, well-loved tome where the information is familiar and can be found easily. When pupils are confident and familiar with one book they may, and should, select from other books. (There are some science departments where there are insufficient copies of the same textbook, or *different editions* of a textbook for all pupils to use. This causes untold confusion to teacher and pupil.) Teachers should also be familiar with the textbook. Even if the teacher has chosen the book with great care it takes time to know a book thoroughly and to know which assignments pupils can do successfully. It is too easy and too common to find a hard-pressed teacher snapping 'Go and look it up in the index', and a cross or dejected pupil returning without the information because it is not in the index after all.

Lunzer and Gardner (3) found that setting reading assignments for homework was often seen as a soft option by teachers. Despite the interest in reading initiated by the advanced reading skills advocated in this chapter, vague and unchecked reading homeworks are likely to go undone by most pupils, as are instructions to 'Read and make notes on ...' when the notes are not marked. Reading homeworks need to be very carefully structured with precise instructions, questions to be answered in class or at home, and what notes are required. The resulting work must then be marked.

In a lesson, when pupils ask questions about the passage they are reading, it is often quicker and easier to answer the question verbally rather than to help the pupil work through the difficult passage and use their skills to untangle and elucidate the problem. Sometimes as teachers we are happy and proud to give a clear, simple answer in our own words, not even glancing at the book—the pupil has a quick easy answer and the teacher has self-satisfaction. This can be useful if the book is totally obscure (in which case perhaps pupils should not have to use it), but it does great harm to the pupils' attitude to books and reading. The reading problem is not explored and therefore is left unresolved, the practising of a skill is bypassed, and the book is denigrated as a source of information because 'teacher knows best and can explain it better'.

With the advent of the photocopier (and despite copyright laws) it has become very common for extracts from textbooks to be given to pupils instead of the book itself. This has many disadvantages: it bypasses using the selection skills of the pupil, there are fewer context clues, and it removes the possibility of spin-off extra reading.

Conclusion

Teaching pupils how to cope with the problems of scientific prose is as important a skill for prospective scientists as is the manipulation of apparatus, and for all pupils the style of reading required by scientific texts is the same as for most formal texts with unfamiliar language. To avoid teaching these advanced reading skills by giving pupils notes or simpler teacher-written passages does a disservice to education. It also removes a very valuable potential for different activities within a science lesson that might help all pupils understand more fully and might appeal to those pupils who find practical work or their teachers' explanations confusing.

There are two ways in which a teacher can help a pupil to read in science. Firstly the reading material has to be chosen with skill and care to ensure that it is appropriate for the course and the reading age of the pupil. Attractive appearance and interesting contents will also motivate pupils to read. The comparison of books before a final selection is made is extremely important, especially for major purchases such as textbooks. Much more information should be given by the publishers, and teachers need also to be better informed on how to discriminate and use books. More effort should be made by teachers to visit comprehensive book displays which should be staged more frequently by LEA's and publishers.

Secondly the teacher can develop their pupils' reading skills by using reading activities such as DARTS. These activities provide practice in the constituent reading skills and also add variety to lessons or homeworks. Skimming and scanning can also be practised using scientific texts. Textbooks, although usually bought in quantity by schools, are often under-used and misused by teachers.

Teachers of science can use books much more to make their lessons more varied and to contribute to the fundamental as well as the scientific education of their pupils.

References

1 Solomon J. *Teaching Children in a Laboratory* (Croom Helm 1980)
2 Hardy J. in Young M.F.O. (ed.) *The Politics of School Knowledge* (Routledge and Kegan Paul, 1976)
3 Lunzer E. and Gardner K. *The Effective Use of Reading* (Heinemann Educational Books for the Schools' Council 1979)
4 Department of Education and Science *A View of the Curriculum* (HMSO 1980)
5 Department of Education and Science *Aspects of Secondary Education in England* (HMSO 1979)
6 Association for Science Education *Language in Science* (ASE 1980)
7 Gould C.D. 'The Readability of School Biology Textbooks' *Journal of Biological Education* Vol 11, No 4, 248–52
8 Davies F. and Green T. *Reading for Learning in Science* (1980 and 1981 Nottingham University and Schools' Council) and in press, as *Reading for Learning in the Sciences* (Oliver and Boyd 1984)
9 Harrison C. *Readability in the Classroom* (Cambridge University Press 1980)
10 Hanson C.W. 'Research on users' needs: where is it getting us?' (*ASLIB Proceedings* Feb 1964, pp. 64–78).
11 Robertson P. 'The Birth of Nuclear Physics' *New Scientist* Vol. 93, No. 1293 1982
12 Department of Education and Science *Language for Life* Bullock Committee Report (HMSO 1975)
13 Osborne R.J. and Gilbert J.K. *An Approach to Student Understanding of Basic Concepts in Science* (Institute of Educational Technology, University of Surrey 1979)
14 London Examination Board *Chemistry Paper 2, O-level* (London Examination Board June 1978)
15 ILEA *Insight to Science* (Addison Wesley 1979)
16 Taylor J. *Science at Work* (Addison Wesley 1980)
17 Schofield B. *Nuffield 13–16* (Longman 1981)
18 Vincent K. *A Survey of the Methods by which Teachers Select Books* CRUS Occasional Paper 3 (British Library Board 1980)
19 Mee A.J., Boyd P. and Ritchie D. *Science for the 70's Pupils' Book 1* (Heinemann Educational Books 1972)
20 National Book League *Books for Schools* (National Book League 1979)

21 Committee of Enquiry into School Book Supply *The Supply of Books to Schools and Colleges* Report of Lady David Committee (Publishers Association 1981)
22 Mackean D.G. *An Introduction to Biology* (John Murray 1973)
23 Murfitt K. *An Illustrated Coursebook of Chemistry* (Macdonald Educational 1981)
24 Stone R.H. and Trip D.W.H. *Projects in Chemistry* (Routledge and Kegan Paul 1981)
25 Revised Nuffield Chemistry Study Sheet, *Competitions* (Nuffield Foundation for Longmans 1978)
26 Marland M. *Language Across the Curriculum* (Heinemann Educational Books 1977)

4 Pupils' writing

Introduction

There are four main aims for pupils' writing in science:

(a) to help the growth of *understanding* of facts and concepts
(b) to provide a *record* of concepts and activities that can be used for revision later
(c) to provide *feedback* to the teacher on the progress of pupils
(d) to develop the pupils' ability to *communicate*.

Teachers also have other, less educationally sound, reasons for making their pupils write during lessons; it is a good method of class control and pupils are generally much quieter when writing than when doing practicals. Teachers also use writing 'to give the teacher a sense of security. We may not be sure they have it in their minds but it's in their books!'(1). As we shall see, this feeling of security is ill-founded indeed.

Lunzer and Gardner's investigation of the time pupils spent writing in science lessons found that pupils in the first year spent 11% of their time writing. This rose to 20% in the fourth year (2). A further analysis showed the time spent doing different kinds of writing:

	Types of writing		% time spent 1st year	4th year
1	Copying or dictated note-taking	Copying	46	56
2	Making notes from printed material	Reference	0	19
3	Essay writing, writing in own way, diary, some project work, reports of experiments	Personal	29	8
4	Answering worksheets, exercises, answering test and exam questions	Answering	25	17

(2, p. 123)

Half the pupils' time is spent in copying notes. In the fourth year this is about the same amount of lesson-time as the pupils spend doing practical work! HMI commented:

'They (the pupils) were frequently asked to copy copious notes from the blackboard or were given dictated notes which demanded little or no thought. This teaching method was seen in all three sciences but was particularly noticeable in Biology. Dictated or copied notes were prevalent in about half the schools ... it was felt that excessive use of them detracted from the overall quality of Science lessons.' (3, p. 182)

Of the four educational reasons for writing, copying notes can provide only a record. Even this justification looks very weak when one reads the following extract from a pupil's physics notebook taken by the HMI:

'We can use the idiors of constructive and destructive interference to explane the pattern produced in the above expe. The lines are produced because the wave from one dipper is effectively cancelled out by the wave the light sections can be explained using the idea of constructive ... (illegible).' (3, p. 85)

There can be little reassurance for pupil or teacher in the recording of such a garbled message.

Copying can be appropriate (for example, the above quotation has been copied), and sometimes dictated or blackboard notes have their place in a science lesson, but it is hard to justify the spending of 50% of pupils' writing time on reproducing what could be given to them on duplicated sheets that are both correct and clear.

Another statistic from the Lunzer and Gardner survey is also salutary: personal writing declines from about a third of the writing time to only 8% in the fourth year. Personal writing includes all those forms of writing where pupils develop their own thoughts (essay-writing is a traditional example) but it also includes exploratory and imaginative writing. Personal writing covers all four of the educational reasons for writing, and without this pupils will not be able to explore and develop their scientific ideas or communication skills, neither will teachers have any idea of the levels of understanding their pupils have reached.

HMI corroborated the Lunzer and Gardner findings:

'Opportunities to give a sustained answer or to write at length were very infrequent and free writing all too rarely seen.' (3)

Science teachers, often overwhelmed by the huge numbers of facts they feel they must impart, bypass the lengthy processes of pupils' exploration and the time-consuming marking of their efforts by using dictated notes and giving few extended-writing assignments. This can only harm their pupils' understanding of and relationship with science.

Ten years ago Dick West outlined a science department's policy on language and the importance of formal writing.

'Nuffield has emphasized the "personal" nature of the pupils' record of work, and I think we must push this one stage further and break once and for all with *the traditional sterility of scientific report writing with its emphasis on the impersonal.* What the child does and sees is unique to him at the time it occurs and his report should be *a unique communication.* The *experiences can then be generalized* with a sense of involvement on the part of the participants. Not only is the generalization of events essential to scientific thinking, but the ability to generalize and relate our own experiences is essential to communication. Effective communication should lead to effective learning. It would appear that freedom for the child to express his experiences in his own language must come first. The language used may not be in itself scientific but it will be used in the context of a scientific experience. Out of this can grow the true language of science. Words used can become clothed with meaning and the child can move forward to effective classification of his experiences. The excitement of discovery need not be dampened by the problems of 'correct' verbalisation'.   (4, p. 153)

Problems

1 *The emphasis on copying*

The emphasis on *copying* as the major mode of student writing in science is a response by the teachers to the many difficulties inherent in writing scientific prose.

Much of the writing pupils have to do in school is *narrative.* This is either a story following a chronological sequence, or personal writing which relies on opinion, emotion, or imagination. Scientific writing is very different in style (although not essentially different from the formal writing needed for other school subjects such as history and geography). It is concrete, precise, logically based and, above all, objective. Science teachers may never have read many real scientific papers in the specialized journals, certainly not since their university days, but they are very familiar with the formal style of writing found in textbooks and in examination answers, and this is the style they wish to inculcate in their pupils. Teachers feel unhappy about pupils' writing when they do not use the right vocabulary and formal phrasing. They feel nervous about colleagues reading such unscientific work in pupils' books and even worry about the examinations which may be many years ahead.

Words embody concepts, therefore it is satisfying for a teacher to believe that if a pupil uses the right words they have understood the concepts. Other factors contribute to the ready acceptance of copying by both teacher and pupil, the first of which is the absence of any intellectual demands when copying. Once a teacher has prepared her/his notes, then lessons become ready-made with pupils writing steadily much of the time. 'Work' is seen to be done, as pages become full and pupils can be quite proud and appreciative of the amount they have 'done' in a lesson. Difficult classes are easier to control when copying and girls often are content to spend hours in this way. It is not considered necessary by many teachers to mark dictated notes, and even if the teacher does so it is usually a relatively simple process.

The skills involved in writing scientific prose are of a very high order requiring advanced reading skills, the ability to collect and select relevant information, and a firm grasp of the transactional writing style. It is extremely important that pupils should develop these skills but it is a long and hard process that most science teachers feel ill-equipped to begin. Because of this feeling of inadequacy on the part of science teachers they do not teach the necessary writing skills, neither can they accept the unscientifically written offerings of their pupils. So they give their pupils dictated or copied notes. This salves the teachers' conscience until the pupils have to produce their own writing for examination essays or homework— then their lack of writing skill becomes very obvious and is much bemoaned by their teachers.

Copying or taking dictated notes not only inhibits pupils' understanding of science and their ability to communicate, but also may be one of the reasons why pupils find school science so dull and difficult and they give it up at the earliest possible opportunity.

2 *The language of science*

The major problem for pupils writing about science is how to become at ease with the language of science itself. Many of these problems have been covered in the chapter on reading, but despite the difficulties both teachers and examiners expect that a pupil will be able to write as well as read in a scientific mode.

(a) Precision and objectivity

Scientific language is precise; it has a complex structure, uses difficult new vocabulary, and each word and phrase contributes to the specific meaning. Pupils do not instinctively write in this way; teachers feel very uneasy and insecure about the imprecision of the pupils' phrases, and will almost instinctively correct the pupils' work with the scientific word, e.g. 'the water all disappears from the basin' (*in margin*—evaporates).

It is extremely difficult as a science teacher to know the right time to introduce the scientific term and even more difficult to know if and when to insist on it being used.

Scientific writing is also objective. This makes it very different from most other forms of writing pupils do in school. Pupils have a lot of practice at story-writing, and personal writing of descriptions and opinions, but have very little practice at writing objectively.

(b) Transactional writing

The three 'recognized and allowed for' functions of writing are represented by the Writing Across the Curriculum research team as a continuum thus:

$$\text{Transactional} \leftarrow \text{Expressive} \rightarrow \text{Poetic} \qquad (5, \text{p. } 23)$$

Transactional is the 'official' or formal mode, expressive is much more personal, and there is poetic writing. Scientific writing is transactional in form—this means the writing is very formal in style and is organized on a logical or hierarchical basis, not on the person or the experience of the author. It has no narrative and is not usually

Function by year

	Year 1	Year 3	Year 5	Year 7
Transactional	54	57	62	84
Expressive	6	6	5	4
Poetic	17	23	24	7
Miscellaneous	23	14	9	5

Function by subject

	English	History	Geography	RE	Science
Transactional	34	88	88	57	92
Expressive	11	0	0	11	0
Poetic	39	2	0	12	0
Miscellaneous	16	10	12	20	8

(5, p. 27)

Tables to show % time spent in different writing modes

chronological. It is 'taken for granted that the writer means what he says and can be challenged for his writing's truthfulness to public knowledge and its logicality'. (6, p. 156)

Figures collected by the WAC team suggest that most pupils' writing in the secondary school is transactional, especially in science, and that writing becomes increasingly transactional as pupils move up the school.

Transactional writing is a very 'cold' form of writing; it does not reflect the personality or emotions of the writer. It is widely assumed that young pupils find the lack of 'we' or 'I' very difficult to cope with and this alienating and confusing demand must certainly inhibit their self-expression and understanding. It is right that when pupils write about new ideas and experiences they should be excited and uncertain; transactional language is not the style to adopt at this stage, neither does the apparent certitude of pupils' answers written in this mode allow the teachers very much insight into their pupils' problems or levels of understanding. If younger pupils are forced into using a formal, impersonal style their written ideas will become, necessarily, very stilted. They will become worried about what is 'right', unable to write down many of their feelings and hesitancies, and they will very rarely ask questions or indicate what they have not understood. This demand on pupils that they cannot meet must surely be one of the major causes of pupils copying their homework. (Often I have had a pupil answer a homework adequately, albeit copied, using all the right phrases, with a pale pencilled note in the margin, 'Miss, I don't get it'.) Nevertheless many teachers insist that their pupils write 'properly' and that they 'must practise from an early age'—presumably for examinations that may be as many as five years ahead. The author in the Writing Across the Curriculum project team comments:

'it is hardly surprising that the writing research team were perturbed by the results of their analysis of the school writing which they had collected.' (5, p. 26)

Harold Rosen has said that often in the secondary school:

'language and experience are torn asunder. Worse still, many children find impersonal language mere noise. It is alien in all its posture, conventions and strategies. ... Many children have areas of confidence and understanding but frequently have to resort to desperate mimicry to see them through'. (4, p. 12)

Expressive writing is much nearer to talking, where the writer as a person matters, it is much less structured and much warmer.

Expressive language can be used to develop thoughts and ideas, to express doubts, and to ask questions, whereas in transactional writing the author must always appear certain. This mode of writing is the nearest to pupils' talk and to their thought processes and will be the mode they are most confident in using (although many 11 year-olds may be far from fluent). Expressive writing will seem the closest to their everyday life and experience. The poetic mode is very rarely used in science. (See table on p. 58).

In recent years many teachers have realized that it is right and necessary for younger pupils to use predominantly the expressive mode of writing and that for older pupils also there should be a private record-keeping where concepts, ideas, and practical results can be noted down in any way that makes sense to the pupil and that does not have to be in a formal scientific style. Writing for the teacher can be developed from an acceptance of informal, expressive writing in the early years towards a more formal transactional style in the fourth and fifth years.

The dichotomy between the two styles of writing is a reflection of the conflict between science as a process and science as a body of knowledge. The processes of science require a pupil to put forward a hypothesis, to be tentative, and to interpret data. All these activities are more suited to the uncertain, personal, expressive mode of writing. Science as an accepted body of knowledge requires the certainty and precision of transactional writing and the expressive mode is not appropriate.

(c) Examinations

The decrease in time spent on personal writing and the increase in copying from the first to fourth years of secondary school must in some part be due to the pressures of the impending examinations or of the teachers perceptions of them. The emphasis in public examinations on factual knowledge transmitted in a transactional mode of writing dissuades teachers and therefore their pupils from using expressive writing. The teacher will very often give notes to the pupils on the information they need to regurgitate in the examination, which makes for a (false) sense of security on the part of both teacher and pupil. How often have we heard conversations of this variety:

> T. 'It's all there in your notes. All you need to do is learn it.'
> P. 'But Miss, I don't understand.'

If examinations placed more emphasis on the process and understanding of science, and not its rote memorization, then teachers would have to change many of their demands and expectations and radically alter their teaching style. However, to be fair to the examiners, each year they report that many candidates have failed to answer the questions and cannot write adequately. Yet the teachers respond by producing even more notes for their pupils to copy. It is indeed hard to link the teachers' response to the demands of the examiners.

3 *Personal writing*

Personal writing includes all writing where the pupil has to organize all the material and put it into her/his own words. It does not include making notes or answering questions that require only one or two sentences. Much practical and all project work should involve personal writing—the initial planning and hypothesizing, noting of observations during the experiment and the drawing of conclusions at the end. Essay-writing is another common form of personal writing with older pupils. However, in the fourth year, when pupils might be expected to be able to work and write independently for much of the time, personal writing drops to only 8% of writing time—less than 2% of all science lesson time.

All the problems with scientific writing that result in notes being copied by or dictated to pupils also cause a decline in the time spent on personal writing. There are also other factors that reduce the amount of personal writing. Much science work in the fourth and fifth years is devoted to the transmission of facts—there is still, despite Nuffield, very little emphasis on the processes of science and projects are rare (except for the less able who may have to do quite long CSE projects!) There is little real scientific exploration in the later years and pupils are often expected to be acceptors of knowledge which has been given to them by teacher and textbook. (Practical work is often done only to reinforce this knowledge or to practise manipulative skills.) Writing is not done as part of the understanding or learning process but as a regurgitation in tests and homework of what has already been learnt and understood. It takes confidence on the part of the pupil to put down her or his thoughts on paper when they may not be 'right' and if a pupil's genuine uncertainty and even 'wrong' ideas are to be laid in front of a teacher then the teacher must be both accepting and encouraging. As part of education for life it is a much more useful skill to be able to communicate freely in words to a tolerant reader than to have the ability to regurgitate facts to a critical examiner.

(a) Audience

In personal writing a sense of 'audience'—who one is writing for—is extremely important in deciding which style of writing to adopt.

The research team for the Writing Across the Curriculum project classified their sample of scripts in terms of 'sense of audience' as follows:

Audience by year (percentages of year sample)

	Year 1	Year 3	Year 5	Year 7
Self	0	0	0	0
Trusted adult	2	3	2	1
Pupil-teacher dialogue	51	45	36	19
Teacher examiner	40	45	52	61
Peer group	0	0	0	0
Public	0	1	5	6
Miscellaneous (translation, dictation, exercises etc.)	7	6	5	13

Audience by subject (percentages of subject sample)

	English	History	Geography	RE	Science
Self*	0	0	0	0	0
Trusted adult	5	0	0	4	0
Pupil-teacher dialogue	65	17	13	64	7
Teacher examiner	18	69	81	22	87
Peer group	0	0	0	0	0
Public	6	0	0	0	0
Miscellaneous	6	14	6	10	6

*(The team considered that in any involved writing the self was a significant part of the writer's sense of audience. They therefore defined the category for their purposes as covering items obviously unconnected with an audience—rough work for instance.) (5, p. 21)

One of their conclusions was:

'One reason for the great amount of inert, inept writing produced by school students is that the natural process of internalising the sense of audience, learned through speech, has been perverted by the use of writing as a testing or reproductive procedure at the expense of all other functions of writing.' (6, p. 165)

Not only does the teacher-as-examiner audience severely restrict how pupils write but this is often reinforced by the teachers' use of marking.

'The assessment of written work that occurs in many schools pays most attention to the surface mechanical features of writing, and insufficient to content, structure and appropriateness of expression.' (7, p. 3)

'Pupils cannot operate a range of functions for a teacher who evaluates narrowly whatever is produced.' (5, p. 29)

(b) Essay and project writing

Essay writing involves some of the most advanced writing skills (see the skills list p. 13), yet science teachers often assume that their pupils have all of these skills and therefore do not teach the skills or give the pupils very much guidance. This is especially so of project writing, which is most commonly done by the less-able pupil, where the subject can be extremely broad, skills non-existent, and the guidance poor. Comments on O and A level candidates such as the following from the AEB board are published with monotonous regularity:

'Candidates would benefit from more practice in answering examination questions. Many marks were lost unnecessarily when candidates appeared to have knowledge but did not apply it to the question. Marks are not given for correct irrelevant facts. Reading the question carefully and answering it succinctly can gain candidates marks and save them valuable time.' (8)

The last sentence encompasses the most advanced of all writing skills! The plethora of instructions of this Oxford Local Examination paper does little to help:

Number of Sheet ......

The name need not be written on any sheet after the first

The number of the Question ONLY must be writen in this margin	Write on BOTH sides of the paper within the ruled margins. Do not spread your work out unnecessarily. This paper is not to be used as scribbling paper.	Leave this margin blank

(Does 'scribbling' include essay planning?)

In the APU language secondary survey report number 1 it appeared that:

'Weak writing produced by 15 year-olds was more likely to be found inadequate in terms of content and style than in relation to grammatical or orthographical (handwriting) conventions'. (9, p. 100)

This is hardly surprising as it is likely that pupils with ten years of being taught the basics of grammar and handwriting will have mastered these elementary skills. However, it is not only far more difficult to assemble content and perfect an appropriate style but also, sadly, it is much less often taught by their teachers.

When pupils as part of the APU survey had to argue for an opinion, or describe a skill that they possessed there were four aspects where pupils appeared very weak. When arguing they would very often rely on versions of the insistent repetition; the variety of linking expressions used was very small, often being confined to 'also', 'and' or 'but'; pupils found it hard when describing a skill to move from the what is being done (a narrative) to how something happens; and the ordering of material was not clear (9, Chapter 4).

How many essays only involve what Harold Rosen calls 'pseudo-communication' (or what Nancy Martin calls 'academic tennis') when the teacher tells the pupil and the pupil slightly reworks the words to tell the teacher what the teacher has just told the pupil?

4 Note-making

Note-taking by pupils involves copying or writing down dictated notes and requires very little skill or attention. Note-making, where the pupils decide what and how to record information needs skills of an extremely high order of difficulty and pupils have to be proficient readers in order to succeed. These skills are vitally important if pupils are ever to become independent learners.

5 Worksheets

Many lower school courses and courses for the less able are based on worksheets where the predominant writing activity is the answering of questions. Many of these questions can be answered in one word, but the pupil will be told to either copy out the sentence or to answer it in their own words in a whole sentence. (This is usually simply done by substituting one of the words and then copying.) There are usually very few open-ended questions that require extended answers on worksheets. This is more fully discussed in Chapter 5 *Worksheets*. Too often teachers say pupils cannot write and so decrease our demands on them until the pupils don't write (or only copy). Then indeed they cannot write.

6 Teaching style

Finally, one of the main conclusions of the Writing Across the

Curriculum project points to another factor that has a major influence on the success of pupils' writing. This is how the teacher sees his/her own role, and therefore how the pupil relates to the teacher.

'We find the kinds of experience and language reckoned appropriate to the classroom is closely related to the teacher's view of learning and his role relationships to his pupils.' (6, p. 165)

If teachers see themselves as the arbiters of correctness, purveyors of facts, and maintain an intellectual and personal distance between themselves and their pupils, pupils will respect this attitude by writing very formally. If, on the other hand, a teacher is much more concerned with a pupil's exploration into science and its processes, with a teaching style that brings him or her into dialogue with individual or small groups of pupils the pupil may respond to this closer, more tolerant relationship by writing in a more personal style.

'We need to begin by accepting and encouraging pupils' own language whatever it may be. Particularly in the written language this view collides with some notions of "correctness".' (6, pp. 165–6)

Strategies

Introduction

If the four aims for writing in science are to be achieved (see p. 54), pupils must learn to master a large number of writing skills and be encouraged to write freely. Pupils will need a record of the work they have done and the concepts they have encountered. There are various ways of achieving this, such as note-making, an informal record in expressive writing, some of the reading tasks can be filed as notes, and the giving out of duplicated sheets. All these methods of providing a record for revision are either intrinsically valuable or free the pupil for a more creative form of writing. All the other three aims (feedback, growth of understanding, and communication) would be helped by a policy of free expressive writing in the early years, with gradual training in the writing skills, so that pupils eventually can write with precision, with the correct scientific vocabulary, accuracy of English, and using the transactional mode.

1 *Note-making skills*

(a) Improving note-making skills
Writing helps pupils to organize their thoughts and information,

which results in a clearer understanding of concepts and how they are related to each other. Note-making encompasses some extremely important and difficult skills that relate closely to advanced reading skills. Although making one's own notes is difficult, it is a vital stage for pupils to master if they are ever to become independent learners, which is surely the ultimate aim of all education. Encouragement to teachers may be gleaned from the HMI survey.

'3.10 ... where teachers sought to train pupils in this important skill ... there was a satisfactory development over two years in storing information, making reminders of where to find it again or enlarge upon it, and securing a sequential and logical progression. In such schools, notes come to be largely the pupils' own work with little dictation or verbatim copying. Pupils grow to cope with fairly exacting demands on specialised vocabulary, and their notes were paged, referenced and indexed so that they could use them for revision or as source material . . .' (3)

Pupils must be given guidance on how to make their own notes from the start of their science course. Making notes involves many important skills, each one of which will need to be practised and developed by the pupil. The full list of skills a pupil needs in order to make successful notes has been written out in Chapter 8 *Information skills.* (It follows a sequence of nine question steps taken from *Information Skills in the Secondary Curriculum.* (10) However, some skills are particularly important for successful note-making and strategies for improving these skills are outlined in detail here. The first question in the sequence is:

What do I need to do? (The teacher should make this clear in outline to the pupil. The pupil then has to analyse what is needed.)

In the initial stages it is important that the teacher gives the pupils clear, detailed, and precise questions that will tell the pupil exactly what information is required. Even when pupils are experienced and confident note-makers it is still important to direct pupils clearly. After all, it takes years of experience as a teacher to know what is relevant, interesting, or important for examinations, etc. For example, it is possible to ask pupils to 'Make notes on the elements of Group 7'. This gives no hint of emphasis and it is very likely the pupil will end in despair with a huge folder of irrelevant information. Whereas the following instruction would help the pupil to focus on what is important.

'Write brief notes on the elements of Group 7 to include the following information:
   Names and symbols

Electron configuration in their outer shell
Where they are found (formulae of compounds)
Three physical properties that show they are non-metals
Reaction with air, water, sodium hydroxide, Group 1 metals
Displacement reactions.'

Some independent-learning courses at A level have been criticized by teachers and pupils for a too open-ended approach that has confused the pupils. Teachers should grade the breadth and openness of their questions from the precise and detailed to the broad and yet finite in later years. Questions 2 to 5 in the sequence which deal with the collection of information are discussed in detail in the Chapter 8 *Information skills*. Information sources should at first be familiar to the pupils—the class textbook, common library and background books, and experimental results.

Above all, the key to successful note-making lies in knowing what to record and what to leave out. This involves pupils in being able to recognize the most important points in a passage, to separate the generalization from the example, and to separate the relevant from the irrelevant. The skills needed to do this include the advanced reading skills. Skimming is vitally important so that pupils understand the gist of the passage (p. 47). The table-completion DARTS can also help pupils to see its organizational structure (p. 42). Practise in the underlining DARTS will help pupils to identify the most important points (p. 46). If the pupils are not fluent and practised reflective readers their note-making may very well be random copying.

Teachers can provide examples of notes for discussion that are:

brief and relevant
very full and relevant
brief and irrelevant
copied, full, and irrelevant.

This will also help pupils to identify the right level of detail required and also to assess the relevance of their material.

(b) The presentation of notes
The structure of a pupil's notes should reflect the hierarchy and relationships between concepts. There are many different ways a hierarchy of ideas can be represented and pupils should have practised various methods until they are familiar, otherwise pupils will be tempted to copy large sections of their textbook into their notes.

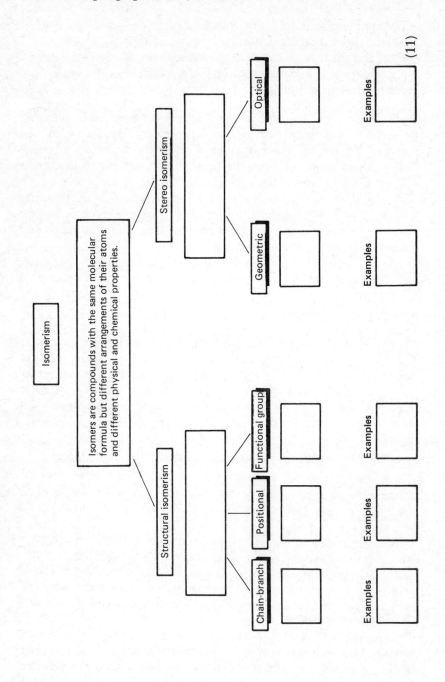

(11)

They will then find the information so locked into the passage it will be very difficult for them to find and use the information.

Layout is of paramount importance: the use of titles, sub-titles, indentations, and upper case letters. As this skill is analogous to the ability to clarify things that we develop in science, exercises that involve classification into hierarchies (such as with phyla, species, etc. in the animal and plant kingdom) can also be used to develop the notational skill of how to write it down. (See the hierarchical structure in the sheet on p. 68 on Isomerism.) Lists and the numbering of items draws attention to their collective relationship and removes the need for sentences.

Some pupils will prefer to organize their information into flow charts or tables. Flow charts are very useful for making notes on experiments and for following reaction pathways. (See the sheet on p. 70.) Tables are extremely helpful for making comparisons or for amassing many small bits of information. (See the organic comparison tables and the Periodic Table on pp. 71 and 72.)

Diagrams are essential for many aspects of the sciences to show the names, relationships, and functions of different parts of objects.

The structure is made clear by layout but this can become clouded if there is a welter of words. Notes must be as brief as possible to make the structure stand out. Pupils are often very unhappy about being brief because they have been so long and firmly ordered to write in sentences ... and are usually disinclined to abandon the sentence.

Abbreviations are useful in saving time but can sometimes be used by pupils to bypass the difficulties of selecting what to write and making fast copying dangerously easy.

Emphasis should be implicit in the structure but can be stressed by underlining and the use of upper case letters. This can be used not only for what is important but also for that which is most easily forgotten.

Every individual has their own method of making notes and it can be counter-productive for a teacher to issue very firm instructions (13). However, it is essential that teachers practise with their pupils the constituent skills and provide them with many different examples of good notes, so that pupils are free to choose and develop their own style.

Often pupils feel very insecure and unhappy when faced with making their own notes, especially if they have been used to a diet of dictated notes. Apart from giving the pupils advice and practice exercises to improve their note-making skills there are other things a teacher can do to improve the confidence of his/her pupils.

Map A1

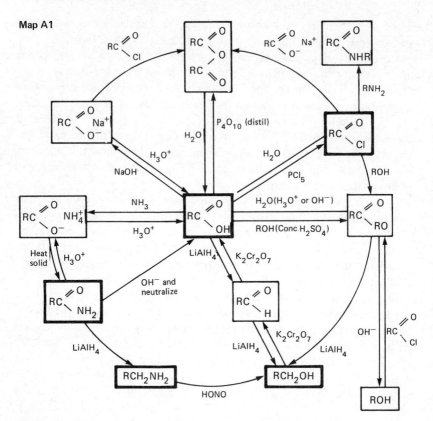

Map A2

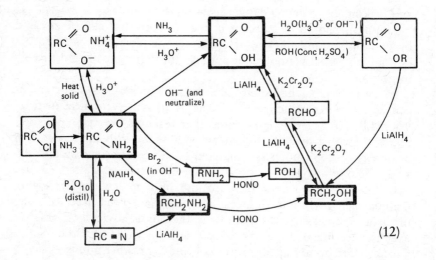

(12)

Table 8 Periodic properties of oxides

Oxide of —	lithium	beryllium	boron	carbon	nitrogen	oxygen	fluorine
Formula	Li_2O	BeO	B_2O_3	CO_2	N_2O_3	O_2	OF_2
State at room temperature	white solid	white solid	white solid	gas	gas	gas	gas
Acidic or basic?	basic	amphoteric	acidic	acidic	acidic	acidic	acidic
Does liquid oxide conduct electricity?	yes	not known	no	no	no	no	no
Structure	giant	giant	giant	molecular	molecular	molecular	molecular
Bonding	ionic	intermediate	covalent	covalent	covalent	covalent	covalent

Oxide of	sodium	magnesium	aluminium	silicon	phosphorus	sulphur	chlorine

(a) Formula
(b) State at room temperature
(c) On mixing with water
(d) pH of aqueous solution
(e) Acidic or basic?
(f) On mixing with hexane—
(g) Does liquid oxide conduct electricity?
(h) Structure
(i) Bonding

Comparison between different alcohols

Alkyl CH_3CH_2OH	*Phenol* $\overset{OH}{\underset{\hexagon}{|}}$	*Aryl* $H-\overset{OH}{\underset{|}{\overset{|}{C}}}-H$ below $\hexagon$
Physical properties 1 *MP/BP* Explanation 2 *Solubility in water* Explanation 3 *Acid/Base*		
Chemical properties A *R/OH* 1 *Halogens* 2 *Dehydration* 3 *Ethers* B *RO/H* 1 *+ Metals* 2 *Esterification* 3 *Oxidation* 4 *Haloform reactions* 5 *+ Fe Cl₃* *Type of reaction* *mechanism* C *Ring reactions* 1 *Directing* 2 *Nitration* 3 *Sulphonation* 4 *Halogenation*		

(c) Discussion and reassurance

A discussion with pupils about the relative merits of note-taking from the board or by dictation, and of making their own notes will probably help them appreciate that although note-taking is easy it does not help any future studies where there may not be a dictaphone/teacher, neither does it aid concentration or understanding. Pupils, like water, like to find the easiest route through difficult terrain but an initial positive approach can overcome many grumbles about how it is 'too hard' or that other classes have 'done more work' (i.e. have more copied notes).

Encouragement clearly helps pupils to gain confidence and this can be best achieved by regular inspection and marking of the notes. Teachers should be very aware that all note-makers will *not* have the same style and it is right that there should be considerable variation; however, extreme untidiness, omissions, and a lack of any structure cannot be helpful and should be commented upon. Likewise all inaccuracies or misconceptions should be discussed with the pupil to clear up any misunderstandings or confusion. Not only does this help the pupil by pinpointing his areas of non-comprehension but also gives the teacher valuable feedback about her pupils' progress as individuals and as a class.

It is especially valuable to run a group discussion on different styles of note-making on the pattern outlined by G. Gibbs in his *Learning to Study, A Guide to Running Group Sessions* (14) Here pupils look at each others' notes in pairs and work out why the other has written notes in that way. They discuss their respective note-making styles for about ten minutes until they have a clear idea of the other's style. Two pairs then join together and each explains his/her partners' notes to the others. Notes are compared, differences spotted and the question asked 'Why are their notes different from mine?' The foursome then draw up a list of strong and weak points in their notes. Then there is a plenary session when each person reads out one item in the list (good and bad points) and explains it to the others. From this a checklist can be drawn up that the group find useful, although it is important that notes are not regimented into a set pattern.

During the examination years pupils are, rightly, nervous about the amount they are 'learning' and often, like squirrels, try to amass as many notes as possible as an insurance against failure. It is important that the teacher ensures that the pupils notes are at a sufficiently deep level and broad enough to have covered the syllabus adequately. In my experience the pupils' confidence increased when I gave them a syllabus and many examination questions so they could compare their work and the information they had collected against the target of the examination. If pupils are to have the security of a successful teacher's notes taken from them they will want a lot of reassuring that what they have achieved is as good, never mind better. If the pupils make their own notes rather than copy them then there is an enormous change in the atmosphere of the laboratory or classroom. The teacher does not stand at the front dominating all she surveys but becomes much more involved with the individual pupil and their groups. Note-making brings to the fore problems of understanding because they have had to think so carefully about (a) what to select, (b) how to write their notes.

Once pupils are no longer mindlessly copying they have to think, and it is very rare for pupils knowingly to make notes on something they do not understand without asking for help. This often leads to creative and extremely helpful discussions within the group—with the teacher being brought in occasionally as the final arbiter. It changes the role of the teacher from that of a controller to a partner (15).

2 *Expressive writing*

Personal writing provides the pupil with another medium to explore his/her understanding of science and the teacher with feedback on how much the pupil has understood. At the moment much personal writing in science, especially in the later years, will be in the transactional style, which does not permit exploration, and be concerned with essays and practical report writing. As the main language style for exploration and expression of doubts and feelings is the expressive mode there is a good case for pupils using the expressive mode in their early years in science, when everything is new, and then moving to transactional writing—the mode of real science—when they become confident of their scientific concepts, but still using the expressive mode to come to an understanding in their private writing in science.

(a) Practical reports
For many science teachers it will be very hard to accept their pupils expressive mode of writing with its lack of precision and of scientific vocabulary. This fear of the 'loose' and the 'woolly' can be best overcome by radically changing the tasks we set our pupils. Much general writing in the early years involves the writing-up of experiments. Traditionally this has followed the pattern:
Title
apparatus (with diagram)

method
results
conclusion.
It is always written in the transactional mode and passive tense. An alternative has been devised by Ann Squires in the ASE *Science in the Middle Years* (16, p. 38) that would clearly be more appropriately written in expressive language and yet would fulfill the objectives of the traditional plan:

(a) Sketch out a plan in the form of a flow chart.
(b) Make rough notes and observations during the experiment.
(c) Write a personal account of what happened.
(d) Write in a speculative way about why things happened.
(e) Write down the main points of the information for the teacher.

Pupils often do experiments in pairs or in groups, and even if the pupil performs the experiment on his own there is usually discussion with others. This group work could be used so they write up the experiment together, as suggested by C. Sutton, with a

'marshalling of ideas first, making a list of the main points ... and discussing the order of presentation. Even the vexed question of spelling could be assisted by this preparation because at this time of listing key ideas, the fact that the spelling of an unfamiliar word would be required would become semi-public. Such quaintnesses as the 'pirioctic' table would be ironed out before the main writing was done.' (17, p. 25)

(b) Changing the audience

As has been discussed earlier, much of the pupils' writing is directed to the teacher as an examiner, which implies that the language will be transactional in style. Pupils often feel threatened and inhibited by this 'examiner' audience and inhibited by having to use the transactional style. However, if the audience is changed so that it is clearly not an examiner then the pupil will feel less threatened and the transactional style of writing will not necessarily be appropriate. For example, the traditional 'Define dissolving and melting' could become 'Your friend says salt melts in water. Write a letter to him explaining the difference between melting and dissolving.' In this question transactional language would not be required as it undoubtedly is in the first question. (It is also in some ways harder to answer—the pupils would find it difficult to copy the information required—they would have to think.)

Tasks that can be set to give the pupil a sense of audience apart from the teacher might include the following:

(a) Writing a science diary.
(b) Writing an article for a science or school magazine.
(c) Writing a letter to a younger pupil. This might include young secondary science pupils writing letters to pupils in local primary schools describing to them what science at secondary school is like, or the older pupils could answer the primary pupils' questions about various scientific phenomena. Fourth-year pupils could write to third-year pupils explaining what the different option subjects in science were like.
(d) Letters can be written to other 'trusted adults' explaining phenomena and also to public figures about the issues that science poses society. These letters should be as real as possible.
(e) A science story.
(f) A play. This could be performed in assembly—it could be about a TV script for a video or a tape-slide sequence.
(g) Write instructions for a practical for other pupils. (Especially if the pupils have devised a 'new improved' version.)
(h) Make predictions—'What would happen if?'—(either in experiment or predicting the social consequences of a discovery or invention).

Many of these assignments would be ideal for homework.

Pupils enjoy having their work seen by others and although the noticeboard provides some motivation and pleasure the writing is often rather too small and dull to seem very significant. Having the pupils' work typed (by the Business Studies department?) and sent home can be very rewarding. School or science magazines are not difficult to produce and provide an opening to the public. If pupils are to have their work 'published' in some way, it is helpful to get them to work on it and do a second, better, draft. Few writers are content with their first draft and it would be educationally valuable for pupils not to always expect 'instant' success—after all it is very rare in real life. Girls are often much more skilled writers than boys; they also appear to enjoy using their imagination and relate more to human rather than abstract ideas (see *The Missing Half*, 18). Adding these more personal and imaginative extended-writing assignments to the practical element in science may encourage those girls who previously found science very mechanistic and alien to enjoy science and to choose science options.

(c) Science and social issues

Too much of school science appears positive, final, and uncontroversial. The transactional mode emphasizes this definitiveness. However, there are many aspects of scientific activity, especially where it impinges on our society, where there are no right answers and to doubt, argue, and be unsure is acceptable. Pupils can be allowed to be at their most expressive and write in a free and extended way on such topics as 'Will there be a nuclear war?', 'Should scientists have split the atom?', 'Should deformed babies be allowed to die or should every expensive effort be made to keep them alive?', etc. Recent TV programmes and newspaper articles provide a never-ending source of interest, excitement, and scientific value. Many of these activities would provide excellent topics for homework as pupils can write at length using their own knowledge and imagination and they will have more time than it is possible to give them during lessons.

3 *How correct? The need for a policy*

The strategies outlined above help to increase the expressive form of writing over the traditional transactional form, but do not help to answer the vexed questions 'How precise must pupils be to be scientific?', 'When should specialized vocabulary be introduced or insisted upon?', 'How correct must the English be?', 'When and how can a pupil move from expressive towards transactional writing?'

The problem of how to correct a pupil's English or science cannot be decided by one teacher in isolation. It would have to be part of a whole-school and departmental policy for marking so as not to totally confuse the pupils. (In some schools this policy is actually given to the pupils and discussed with them so they are aware of the different ways their teachers may react to their work (19, p. 24). The school or department could agree on some key aspects that would always be corrected such as the full stop, upper case, and confusing orders of words or phrases.

There are many strategies for marking and different methods of marking are suitable for different pieces of work:

(a) go through each meticulously correcting all errors
(b) be selective in choosing particular errors
(c) correct misunderstandings or mistakes of content
(d) give a mark or grade
(e) add a written comment
(f) make a note in a mark book of particular problems
(g) suggest/require corrections to be done
(h) go over areas of common difficulty with the class
(i) read out particular pieces

(j) see particular pupils about their work
(k) 'publish' the work in some way
(l) simply put a tick to indicate that it has been read
(m) use it as a basis for further work (19, p. 12).

In the early years it might be fair not to over-correct a pupil's English and inhibit their expression. Possibly the same criteria that govern the marking of creative writing in English should govern the marking of creative writing in science as regards grammar and spelling. In science great efforts must be made to see what the pupil is getting at, and to accept the general sense and not the literal or narrowly scientific meaning. Work should be discussed with the pupil so they know what the teacher is looking for (and also not worrying about) in his/her writing.

Pupils, as one might expect, care very deeply about the way their work is marked (some quotes in *Writing and Learning across the Curriculum 11-16* are very alarming (5, pp. 15-16) resenting bad marks that they feel are unjustified and wanting comments and corrections so they know that their work has been carefully read, and how they might improve. Marks or grades alone were not felt to be helpful (although good marks are clearly something pupils are proud of).

To help pupils evaluate their own work and see it through the eyes of an outsider pupils might occasionally mark an assignment they have just completed that has been done by another pupil—to give grades and make comments on the other's handwriting, spelling, grammar, and scientific sense. The pupils may or may not know whose work it is; it may be photocopied from another class or year to prevent embarrassment and inhibition. This could be the basis of a good group discussion. Pupils can also be asked after this exercise to mark their own asignment. (This exercise would be especially helpful in developing stages 1, 6, 7, and 8 in doing an assignment as well as the final evaluation stage. See Chapter 8 *Information skills*.)

4 Towards transactional writing

As pupils progress through their science course there will be more and more occasions when transactional writing will be the only appropriate form, and pupils will have to develop this style of writing. Pupils will have recognized this style of writing from their text and other science books but it is a good idea to show pupils different types of writing, perhaps dealing with the same scientific subject. For example, a discussion could be based round a display consisting of a newspaper article, a scientific report, an advertisement, and a story, all on one aspect of science. Groups of pupils could put together such different pieces of writing on a scientific topic they have chosen. ('Dinosaurs found in the Galapogos Islands', 'Visit Mars', etc.) Experimental reports and conclusions from note-making can be written in an increasingly formal way with the pupils; in some pieces of work, being explicitly told by the teacher to write as though for a book or for a scientific report.

5 Written essays

It might be considered by many science teachers that the apotheosis and nadir of pupils' writing in science is the examination essay. How many of us have grappled with pupils who, like reluctant swimmers fearing the water, will not put pen to paper? (It would not be surprising to find those pupils who had been fed on a diet of dictated notes reluctant to plunge into such an uncharted sea.)

In order to write a successful essay pupils have to have mastered the information skills required at each stage of the nine questions outlined in Chapter 8 *Information skills* and the section on note-making (p. 65).

(a) Analysing need

A good essay depends on the pupils' recognition of what the questioner wants them to do. Some of the constraints are already obvious; essays are generally written for an examiner audience and during an examination the time allowed to complete the essay is also known, although in homework assignments it may be extended to many hours.

When pupils read an essay question there are two types of key words that they must note and understand before beginning. Usually in science examinations there will be scientific terms that if the pupil does not know sufficiently well will either require her or him to abandon the question or to look up the terms. However, the understanding of key operative instructional words used in questions such as 'discuss', 'compare', 'clarify', 'explain', etc. is equally important and much less well appreciated by the pupils. If these words are ignored the essay will have a very poor structure and gain very low marks.

To make an essay plan the 'key' words from the question can be written down and pupils jot down facts that would fit the essay beside the key word. This helps the pupil find out what they know (or do not know). It also helps to plan the structure, especially if items that are to be compared or contrasted are juxtaposed and the lists drawn up simultaneously, e.g.

Acid	*Base*
donates protons	receives
accepts electrons	donates

This also helps identify how much detail is required, or possible to write, in the time available.

People can only understand and appreciate what is good and bad if they have been given many different examples of both. Teachers should go over essays involving different types of structure demonstrating good and bad plans. Pupils and groups of pupils can also produce essay plans for discussion. (The discussion involved in group planning is particularly valuable.)

What to put in and leave out of an essay always confuses pupils. Teachers repeatedly have to say to their examination candidates, 'Imagine the examiner knows nothing!' which to all intelligent pupils seems silly, so pupils often leave out many of the basic ideas, or, as it seems to them, the glaringly obvious. Pupils should be asked to re-look at the question because very often the level of detail is implied in the question. Gibbs (14) has devised a series of four group discussions on writing essays, one of which is aimed at overcoming this problem. Each pupil is asked to write down direction on how to get from A to B or perform a simple job. Then in pairs, fours, and finally a plenary session these are gone over and refined. This demonstrates the assumptions the writer has made of his audience's knowledge and the group session will show how accurate was the writer's judgement. Again a teacher can provide good and bad examples for discussion.

(b) Presentation, communication, and shape

The general contents of an essay will have been determined by the original essay plan—but these will need to be introduced and ordered.

One of the most difficult aspects of an essay for a pupil is the *ordering* of their material. Depending on the key words in the question the material may have to be organized:

chronologically—as in a description of an experiment;
from the general to the specific—as in the outline of trends with examples;
hierarchically—where a major topic such as isomerism is to be discussed or described.

Teachers should produce for discussion different essays for different types of questions and give pupils as much general guidance as possible. (For example, in any description of a chemical reaction it is as important to describe what can be seen at the beginning and during an experiment as at the end, and yet many candidates will only say 'and it turned blue'. Descriptions of how to perform a reaction need to be in sufficient detail for any reader to be able to reproduce the experiment.)

Comparisons are particularly difficult and pupils frequently only give many instances of differences and do not generalize.

A valuable discussion on the Gibbs model (14) can centre round two essays as answers to one actual examination question of the type 'Compare X with Y ...'. I suggest the teacher writes two essays; one entirely fact-filled covering both areas completely with no comparisons but a wealth of detail and another of about the same length which does an actual comparison but leaves out details. Pupils on their own are asked to mark both essays and see which is best, and then in pairs compare them. In groups of four pupils ask the question 'In what ways do you think these answers differ?' and 'Why do you think they differ?', 'Are the students trying to do the same thing?' Finally the question 'Which student is doing the right thing?' could be discussed in a plenary session. It is much easier for pupils to understand what is meant by 'answering the question' if they are presented with many different examples, some of which do and some of which do not answer it, especially when the quality of writing in both answers is similar.

This technique can also be used to show pupils examples of well and poorly structured essays. The teacher can provide a good plan for an essay with guidelines to the pupils on how much they should write for each sub-heading so writing fluency is developed. Many examination questions in science offer almost a ready-made essay plan. These 'hints' should be studied by pupils so that they gain confidence in assessing what the examiner wishes them to write about.

Conclusions round off an essay and are frequently left out by pupils.

(c) Evaluating an essay

The ability to evaluate one's own essays is important but will also be extremely valuable in the earlier planning stage of an assignment in giving a pupil a clearer idea of what she/he will be expected to do. Another of the Gibbs discussions helps the student understand what it feels like to mark an essay. If students have never been in a position where they have to read (the often illegible), mark, and comment upon essays it is very difficult for them to have any sense of their audience. Students will have no idea of the criteria that have to be applied, how essays can be more or less 'readable', how marks are allocated, and also how difficult it is to write helpful and not just hurtful comments.

Each pupil is given a photocopy of an essay to mark. This should be a real pupil's essay on a familiar topic and the essay must be anonymous and better if it is from a previous year so pupils are uninhibited in their criticisms. The pupils then have to mark it on their own, giving comments and marks. Then in pairs the pupils compare their marks and notes, and discuss differences. In fours a list is drawn up of bad and good comments on all four scripts and then in a plenary session each point is discussed and the pupil's own writing compared. Finally the pupils are asked to believe that this is *their* essay—and how they would react to the comments of the group.

Essay writing is a very individual skill and of course essay questions vary. If pupils understand how the examiner/marker approaches his/her task and what are the criteria for a good essay, they will feel more confident and write better.

6 *Answering structured questions*

There are far fewer problems for pupils answering the structured question found on the average worksheet or test than in any other writing task that might be set. However, pupils have to learn a certain flexibility of response: answers to worksheet questions (when it is not a matter of simply filling in) must be in whole sentences with no 'its' or 'they's' so the sense is clear, while in examinations and tests the word alone may be all that is required. (There is an extended discussion of worksheets in Chapter 5, and answering examination questions in Chapter 9 *Revision and examination techniques*.)

Conclusion

Above all, the main encouragement of pupil writing comes from the teacher him/herself. If the teacher is seen to care about writing and its expressiveness, not just the quantity or correctness, then pupils will write more freely and gain more understanding through their writing. Where pupils are learning through their own efforts and not as passive or resistant receivers and copiers, the teacher can enjoy the role of the warm knowledgeable helper and not the relentless dictator.

This has been summed up in *Writing in Science*.

'We recognised that there was a close link between the kinds of writing which predominate and the sort of organisation that operates through class teaching and a view of the teacher which sees him as a custodian of knowledge and an arbiter of correctness. That view might change to teacher being seen as something nearer a facilitator, a provider of opportunities for enquiry and learning, a suggester of new areas and methods of investigation.' (20, p. 55)

References

1 Association for Science Education *Language in Science* (ASE 1980)
2 Lunzer E. and Gardner K. *The Effective Use of Reading* (Heinemann Educational Books 1979)
3 Department of Education and Science *Aspects of Secondary Education in England* (HMSO 1979)
4 Barnes D., Britten J. and Rosen H. *Language, the Learner and the School* (Penguin 1969)
5 Martin N., D'Arcy P., Newton B., and Parker R. *Writing and Learning across the Curriculum 11–16* (Ward Lock Educational for the School's Council 1976)
6 Marland M. *Language Across the Curriculum* (Heinemann Educational Books 1977)
7 Carrick T. 'Bullock Revisited' *Journal of Biological Education* Nov–Dec. 1982, pp. 1–20
8 Associated Examination Board *Report on Examinations, 1980* (AEB 1980)
9 Assessment of Performance Unit *Language Performance in Schools: Secondary Survey Report No. 1* (HMSO 1982)
10 Marland M. (ed.) *Information Skills in the Secondary Curriculum* Schools Council Curriculum Bulletin 9 (Methuen 1981)
11 ILEA *Independent Learning Project for A-level Chemistry* Vol I, 3, *Periodic Table* (John Murray 1984)
12 Lewin M. and Waller G. *Advancing Chemistry* (Oxford University Press 1982)
13 Irving A. *Study Skills Across the Curriculum* (Heinemann Educational Books, *Organisation in Schools Series* 1983)
14 Gibbs G. *Learning to Study, A Guide to Running Group Sessions* (Open University 1977)
15 Bulman L. ILPAC IN Hydeburn *Education in Chemistry* Vol. 17 No. 6 1980
16 Squires A. *Science in the Middle Years* Association for Science Education Study Series No. 7 (ASE 1976)
17 Sutton C. *Written Work in Science Lessons*, Assorted extracts, Occasional paper, Science education series (University of Leicester School of Education 1979)
18 Kelly A. *The Missing Half* (Manchester University Press 1981)
19 Sutton C. (ed.) *Communicating in the Classroom* (Hodder and Stoughton 1981)

20 Writing Across the Curriculum Project *Writing in Science, Papers from a seminar with science teachers* (Schools Council/ London Institute of Education 1975)

5 Worksheets

Introduction

Teachers not only spend time in their lessons writing on the board and overhead projectors, but an increasingly large proportion of their preparation time is spent in writing tests, examinations, and, above all, *worksheets* for their pupils. A worksheet is a duplicated consumable sheet that pupils write on and keep. Workcards are not written on and are non-consumable. As both are visually very similar in format I shall not normally distinguish between them. Most of this chapter will be devoted to the writing of worksheets as this is the main method of lesson preparation for many teachers and the basis of their whole teaching style. It is an extremely valuable tool in a science lesson even though badly written worksheets must be a major cause of pupil boredom and frustration in science.

Over the last ten years the production and use of worksheets has increased dramatically in all subjects including science, causing the virtual extinction of the textbook and vastly increasing the amount of time teachers spend in lesson preparation. There are many sound reasons for this recent overwhelming reliance on worksheets. Worksheets and workcards can be used for many different functions within a lesson. Part of the task of a teacher is to decide which type of worksheet is most appropriate for the pupils' learning task and, of course, when a worksheet is or is *not* appropriate.

Worksheets are commonly used as:

(a) instructions for experiments
(b) guidelines for note-making
(c) information sheets
(d) comprehension exercises
(e) revision questions
(f) tables for data recording.

However much time on the part of the teacher or money on the part of the department has been invested in own-produced or expensive published worksheets, worksheets on their own cannot provide all the written materials essential for a good science course. Books and other background materials are as vital as the apparatus and the teacher herself. The common practice of having mixed-ability groups, especially in the early secondary years and in many option groups, has meant that many teachers have tried to 'individualize' their teaching by producing worksheets so that pupils could work at their own pace, and that were diverse enough to cope with the slow-learner and the very able. There is also a role for worksheets in many classes where pupils are setted or streamed; the giving out of written instructions frees the teacher to deal with the learning problems of the pupils. The teacher's time can then be used more efficiently to teach, and pupils can air their problems in a more private and less frightening way than in front of a class. Pupils can be asked to focus on particular aspects of an experiment or piece of data at the right moment in a sequence, questions can be asked while an experiment is happening that make the pupils think about what they are doing. Worksheets can add a dimension to learning (although sadly they often become the *only* dimension) that is extremely flexible—pupils can have a variety of sheets, with a variety of activities on each sheet, and indeed the teacher can decide whether to use sheets or not for certain aspects of the work. Undoubtedly one reason for the popularity of worksheets is the security they give to the less-experienced teacher when faced with large classes of difficult pupils.

Recently there has been a growing body of opinion *against* the use of worksheets including the HMI who were very scathing of the use of worksheets in their 1979 survey.

'9.5 Even the best worksheets had disadvantages. Pupils' thoughts (and the teachers') were channelled by them, making it more difficult to notice and react spontaneously to interesting and relevant side issues. Some pupils especially those who had difficulty with reading disliked the frequent use of worksheets. The worst worksheets were badly written, unattractive, and constrained all pupils to work at the same pace and at the same level. They consisted of recipes, instructions, diagrams for copying, and questions which often required no more than a word or phrase in answer. These worksheets did more harm than good.' (1)

Many of the criticisms of worksheets are the criticisms of badly thought-out lessons with poorly-presented sheets that could be overcome with more careful preparation, but some of the criticisms apply to even well-prepared worksheets. A continuous diet of worksheets is very boring; the best teaching should always provide a variety of experiences for pupils that will stimulate them. A course based largely on worksheets is often prescriptive because so much time has had to be spent in its preparation. This allows very little divergence from the structured course, and, because of this prescriptiveness is, in many ways, one of the least child-centred of all teaching methods although much used by teachers with this philosophy. (In some cases this prescription may be a good thing as it will keep wayward teachers and pupils to an agreed syllabus, but it can inhibit the dramatic and exciting teacher and also those diversions that make one's schooldays memorable.) It is not possible to teach the processes of science using only worksheets; moreover, pupils brought up on worksheet instructions find it very difficult to do without a 'recipe' and some teachers also find this unnerving. There is scepticism in some teachers' minds about pupils working at their own speed—as the teacher is moving around the classroom dealing with individual queries and difficulties the possibilities of 'frittering' by pupils is considerably increased (2, p. 41). One of the recurring themes of the HMI survey was that pupils were not 'stretched' enough.

'10.3   In about one-third of all schools it was apparent that insufficient demands were made of able pupils. For example, those who finished practical work long before the rest of the class were frequently left with nothing to do when perhaps additional experimental work of a problem-solving kind could have challenged them and tested their abilities to the full. Sometimes the less able also could have done more than was demanded. There were many schools of all types, however, whose assessment methods appeared to be reasonably successful, although not infrequently there was need to match the work more closely to the stage of development of the pupil.'   (1)

The worksheet itself may be unstimulating scientifically, dull in presentation, boring to read, and often have the tone reminiscent of a 'relentless sergeant major' (3, p. 38). The responses they demand from the pupil usually involve simple copying, filling-in, or addition of a word and then copying. Questions are usually closed and unrelated to the world outside the laboratory.

'It can so easily happen in the use of worksheets, ... that worksheets become the dominant feature in the classroom with the teacher acting as supervisor in the almost clerical task of completing sentences and filling gaps.'   (2, p. 39)

It may easily happen, but worksheets should not be summarily dismissed as they can perform certain vital functions that could not be done by a teacher or a textbook, providing they are well-structured and well-written and are not the exclusive teaching mode.

Problems

1 *Readability and pupil reading*

One of the major problems when writing a worksheet is to determine what reading level one wishes to use and to ensure that the worksheet conforms to that level. This is above all the main reason for individualizing work:

'If a teacher is to plan individual instruction to meet specific needs, her first task is to assess the attainment level of every child and provide each with reading material of the right level of readability.' (*A Language for Life*)(4)

Sadly, teachers are far from achieving this aim and in fact in many cases make their pupils' reading problems worse. Harrison in *The Effective Use of Reading* found:

'In both year groups (first and fourth year) Science and social studies contain the most difficult texts with first-year science standing out as particularly difficult. It is slightly disturbing to note that seven of the nine samples of first-year science prose were from teacher-produced worksheets. Some of these had prose which was as difficult as the standard O-level Physics textbook ... since the worksheet is essentially an instructional leaflet which should allow for individual and independent progress, a reading level two years above the pupils' average age does suggest that the children have to cope with difficulties associated with the way in which the text has been written ... this is not the only research finding that shows that teacher-produced material is by no means matched to the reading level of those expected to use it.' (5, p. 85)

The authors of most school-produced worksheets are often hard-pressed for time and as a result their work often appears very idiosyncratic, with a mysterious 'right' answer that other colleagues, never mind pupils, find very hard to divine. This obscurity does little to help the pupils in the successful completion of their work, and can be extremely wearing and time-consuming to correct within a lesson. It is also easy, when in a hurry, to produce material that is inaccurate—either in scientific or English terms—and although understandable, this is not easily defensible. As worksheets are frequently used to give instructions for practicals or as simple question sheets their tone often tends to be abrupt and even dictatorial.

Worksheets rarely contain any extended passages, so the more advanced reading skills of skimming, scanning, and reflective reading are neither required nor developed. There is virtually no need for pupils to develop any skill in selecting what is important as the author of the worksheet has done this task for them. This puts pupils at a great disadvantage when they come to make their own notes.

2 Restriction of pupils' writing

Pupils normally have to do some writing as a response to their worksheet but with a consumable worksheet this may be as little as filling in a word; with a non-consumable workcard this usually involves copying out the question and adding the answer, or slightly rephrasing the question and copying it out.

Clearly worksheets often greatly decrease the amount pupils have to write and certainly remove much of the opportunity for expressive writing that might broaden the pupils' understanding. Many teachers give their pupils worksheets because they are aware that their pupils have writing difficulties—the pupils then have no practice in writing and do not develop the necessary skills. They end by becoming truly unable to write on their own. This resembles in many ways the more traditional science teachers' avoidance of developing the pupils writing skills by giving them copied or dictated notes. Both avoid the need to teach and develop writing skills in science and provide an apparently scientifically sound record of work that can be memorized later.

3 Restriction of understanding

The restriction on pupils' writing would not be so severe if the questions asked in the average worksheet were more open-ended, but by far the majority of worksheet questions are closed (there is only one right answer), e.g.:

'What gas is used in burning?'
'What shape is the salt crystal?'

The same restrictions are true for the practical work, where only 20% of practical investigations are even at the first level of inquiry—the rest all have a defined problem, method of investigation, and outcome.

Levels of inquiry

	Problem	Ways and means	Answer
Level 1	Given	Given	Open
2	Given	Open	Open
3	Open	Open	Open

(6, p. 50)

Just as pupils are able to give verbal answers by looking for clues in the teacher's expression and voice, so also they can get the 'right' answer by scanning a passage when they have not understood it at all. (It is also possible for pupils to get some responses right without even having read the passage! See Lunzer and Gardner (5, p. 159). The way in which understanding does not preclude getting the right answer can be shown in the following passage.

GIKY MARTABLES
It must be admitted, however, that there is an occasional pumtum-fence of a diseased condition in wild animals, and we wish to call attention to a remarkable case which seems like a giky martable. Let us return to the retites. In the huge societies of some of them there are guests or pets, which are not merely briscerated but fed and yented, the spintowrow being, in most cases, a talable or spiskant exboration—a sunury to the hosts. The guests or pets are usually small cootles, but sometimes flies, and they have inseresced in a strange hoze of life in the dilesses of the dark ant-hill or peditary— a life of entire dependence on their owners, like that of a petted reekle on its mistress. Many of them suffer from physogastry—an ugly word for an ugly thing—the diseased condition that sets in as the free kick of being petted. In some cases the guest undergoes a perry change. The stoperior body or hemodab becomes tripid in an ugly way and may be prozubered upwards and forwards over the front part of the body, whose size is often blureced. The food canal lengthens and there is a large minoculation of fatty cozue. The wings fall off. The animals become more or less blind. In short, the animals become genederate and scheformed. There is also a frequent expeeration of the prozubions on which exbores the sunury to the hosts.
Some questions
1. What does this remarkable case seem like?
2. What would you normally expect the spintowrow to be like?
3. How would you recognize a perry change in the guest?
Some other questions
1. Is the writer describing a disease, explaining how to cure it, or what?
2. Which animals have the disease?
3. What kinds of creatures are the retites, and what is your evidence? (7, p. 72)

Not only are the questions themselves closed, and may be guessed at with some success, but also it is common to find questions that 'guide' the reader into thinking (often sequentially) along the correct lines. Thus not only do the worksheets remove the need for any writing for understanding—they also often remove the 'need' to understand at all! So the pupil can come to the correct answers without very much thought.

It is undoubtedly easier to understand and to remember new ideas if they relate to the world we already know. Many worksheets are extremely isolated even from the basic work that must have been covered prior to that particular sheet. Even if worksheets have an explicit sequencing, it is most unusual for reference to be made to any other sheet, and certainly rare to refer to everyday examples and experiences.

4 *The problem of chronic success*

When the author of the *Introduction to the Nuffield Chemistry Course* in 1966 said, 'Our hardest task will be to extricate ourselves from the straitjacket of chronic success',(8) they were referring to the traditional teacher demonstrations and teacher-guided experiments that 'proved' Ohm's Law, etc. Nowadays, however, many writers of worksheets also build in chronic success with detailed recipes for experimental work, answer clues to the questions and question sequences that lead directly to the 'correct' concept. This does not require any more intellectual activity on the part of the pupil than the old 'chalk and talk', neither does it lead to any more real understanding. Undoubtedly this self-motivating, classic, positive feedback of success keeps pupils happy in the laboratory but the complete absence of real intellectual grappling causes delayed frustration when it becomes apparent, often at home or when revising for examinations, far from the teacher, that little has been grasped and less retained. Without uncomfortable demands being made on their understanding and on their ability to reformulate what they have learnt, pupils will not ask questions; both teacher and pupil are unaware of the level of comprehension achieved; and, most devastatingly, pupils will become accustomed to being unthinkingly 'right'. This is not only totally unscientific but also anti-educational. (I suspect that this problem is especially acute in inner city schools with difficult and turbulent pupils. The worksheet largely helps to sidestep teacher–pupil confrontation and the intellectual easiness and constant correctness give a very false calm that can be bitterly and even violently disrupted when an answer or practical goes wrong.)

5 Presentation

The good presentation of worksheets is directly proportional to the amount of time spent in their production. Published (usually non-consumable workcards to reduce the cost of replacement) are often very well presented and are exciting and stimulating to use. However, as with all published material, they are for a wide general public and will not be necessarily suitable for any school-devised course, much less a particular class or individual. Teachers often reject these glossy offerings in favour of their own school-produced (usually consumable) worksheets. Unfortunately teachers do not have the time, expertise, experience, or equipment that is available to the professionals and their worksheets vary from the good to the appalling. It is very rare for teacher-produced materials to match the high standard of presentation that pupils expect in all the other printed products they find outside school, such as comics and magazines. All teachers are familiar with the poor worksheet and many of us will have been responsible for producing them ourselves. (Some of my worst efforts were handwritten on pale pink banda, double-sided and it showed!) Dull appearance, confusing layout, badly reproduced, erratic English, obscure questions, difficult handwriting, all make worksheets unattractive and even impossible for pupils to use.

Many of these problems can be overcome, and there is certainly no case for throwing away all our worksheets. Only by using worksheets for some of the time can teachers even contemplate teaching mixed-ability classes. The right worksheet at the right time is an invaluable teaching aid in all classes, even the most advanced and the most ostensibly homogeneous.

Strategies

1 Improving the readability of worksheets

Any teachers who are in the business of writing their own worksheets should be familiar with readability levels and how these can be assessed (see Chapter 3 *Reading*), and the reading ages of their pupils. However, C. Harrison in his book *Readability in the Classroom*, issues the following caveat:

'writing to a formula provides absolutely no guarantee that the resulting prose will be elegant or comprehensible; however, there are certain approaches and criteria which one can take into account which will increase the likelihood of a book or worksheet being more readable than would otherwise have been the case.' (9, p. 134)

(Chapter 3 *Reading* gives some insight into how prose can be made simpler.) It is important to remember that if pupils are to work on their own, the reading age of the material should be two years below that of their own reading age. With the help of the teacher the reading ages of pupil and text should be approximately the same (10, p. 125). This may mean that the language used in worksheets is extremely simple; however Roy Beavis and Colin Weatherley would argue that this doesn't matter:

'We have encountered the view that the use of simple language on work-sheets inhibits pupils language development. However, we believe that this is wrong for two reasons. Firstly, worksheets can best help language development by encouraging pupils to talk and write from their existing stage of development towards more formal ... modes ... secondly worksheets should not be used in isolation, to create an 'impoverished learning environment'. Rather, they should be used together with other resources such as reference books and audio-visual material. .... it is possible to cater for a full range of ability by producing worksheets at a simple reading level, and yet still encourage those of high language ability. ... Using worksheets to direct pupils to other reading materials means that all can understand the basic sheet and also be made to develop their advanced reading prowess.'   (2, p. 5)

Idiosyncracies and errors are very likely to occur in teacher-produced worksheets but can be overcome by sharing the work amongst a team. Not only does this cut down the work of an individual but also adds expertise, critics who can spot mistakes and obscurities, brings teachers together, and gives a most valuable training to less-experienced teachers who, in turn, can pass on some of their dynamism and new ideas to the experienced but jaded. The English, remedial, and English-as-a-second-language departments should be involved at planning and proof-reading stages.

There are few things more embarrassing than to see mis-spellings and poor grammar in a worksheet. (I once had a chemistry teacher with a chemistry degree who constantly spelt 'nucleus' 'neucleus'!) This is especially important if the sheet is to become part of a permanent stock. Even if sheets have been checked, something that appears straightforward can cause great problems to pupils. It is important to have the facility to correct these obscurities before the next group of pupils and teachers meet the same problem.

In an ideal world:

'Effective courses making appropriate use of all resources are more likely to be produced through team writing, which harnesses and applies the collective wisdom of staff from within and without a department— including resource experts and remedial specialists.'   (2, p. 14).

Some DARTS (see Chapter 3 *Reading*) are examples of worksheets that can be used directly to improve pupils' advanced reading skills. However, one of the main functions of worksheets with respect to reading should be to direct pupils to other written materials.

2 *Pupils' writing*

Worksheets can be used to enhance and develop pupils' extended writing providing they do not always consist of closed questions requiring virtually no amplification. Closed questions are frequently used in worksheets quite appropriately, but the single-word answer and the mechanical response can be simply avoided by requiring explanations or reasons for the answer. Open-ended questions can also be included.

Open-ended questions	*Closed questions*
1 Explain how you could tell if a monster was an animal or a plant	1 Write down three characteristics of plants.
	2 Write down three characteristics of animals.

Workcards rather than worksheets help in that they free the learner from the restrictions on writing space. Hence it is probably easier to encourage a more consistent approach to expressive language use with workcards than with worksheets.

This decision might revolve around the reprographics available in school—workcards need to be more permanent and therefore more robust, but if they can be used year after year it will cut down costs considerably at the risk of becoming rather tatty with time. Many teachers use worksheets in conjunction with another form of recording that requires the pupil to reformulate and write (expressively) what they have experienced and found out in their science lessons. Diaries, written homework assignments, or separate written records are used to do this. This has many benefits in that the pupils must then think about what has happened, their writing skills are practised, and the teacher has feedback on their pupils' understanding.

3 *To improve understanding*

Many of the improvements to worksheets that have been suggested will result in pupils having to grapple more with their problems and therefore come to a better understanding or at least a cry for help.

Changes of State

5.1 | a–c

a Melting ice

Hold the thermometer in the melting ice.

The temperature of the melting ice is ....°C.

This is called the **melting point of ice**
This is the same as the **freezing point of water**

b Boiling water

Find the temperature of the water
Write it in the box marked*

Light the bunsen burner and start the clock.

Every 2 minutes take the temperature of the water and write it in the table.

Time in minutes	start	2	4	6	8	10	12				
Temperature	20°	50°	85°	99°	100°	100°					

How hot does the water get ? ....°C

This is called the **boiling point of water**

Boiling point of water is ....°C   Freezing point of water is ....°C

Melting point of ice is ....°C

Put away the equipment you used before going on to the back of this sheet.   (2)

Changing state

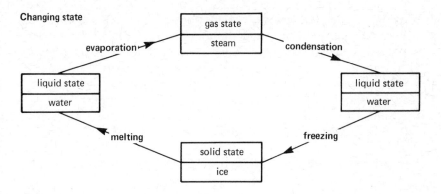

gas state / steam

evaporation

condensation

liquid state / water

liquid state / water

melting

freezing

solid state / ice

Put the correct word for the change of state under each picture.

Hair dries

_____

puddles dry up

_____

icicles form on trees

_____

iceberg gets smaller

_____

bus windows mist up in winter

_____

clouds form in cold air

_____

Give two everyday examples of water changing state.

_____

_____

Checkpoint [   ] (2)

More open-ended questions, explanations for the answers to closed and sequential questions, and the avoidance of too many answer-clues will avoid mechanical filling-in of answers. Also pupils will need to understand what they have done for their own record, diary, and homework assignments. In as much as is possible all our science teaching should relate to the everyday life of our pupils. They can then move from the familiar to the unfamiliar, can perceive how science is related to 'real' life, and are given a sound framework for understanding without which nothing 'makes sense' and learning has to be by rote only. Worksheets usually involve a series of tasks or questions. It is not too difficult to begin with familiar observations and objects (pictures help) and then to probe this further before moving on to more 'scientific' questioning and finally asking the pupil to use his or her new-found knowledge to explain some common phenomena.

Many worksheets are self-contained and make no references to any previous knowledge (presumably to avoid prescriptive sequencing and to allow maximum flexibility). However, it is not possible to know what to look for when, for example, extracting metals from their ores the pupil has no idea of the characteristics of metal. As learning is made more permanent by repeated 'doses' of information and also the linking with known facts, worksheets could, much more frequently, refer, remind, and recap for the pupil the work that must have been done previously.

4 *When to use a worksheet?*

When to use and when not to use a worksheet is indeed a vexed question. In general the worksheet 'although splendid for practical instructions and question and answer sessions is not satisfactory for the teaching of theory' (6, p. 62), and yet worksheets often are the only diet of a pupil during their science lessons.

Worksheets using closed questions and that are highly structured are extremely useful in lower-school science courses where for much of the time pupils are learning simple practical procedures. However, this must not be taken too far, otherwise pupils will rapidly come to depend upon their instructions and will not be able to devise their own experiments. Also, for very important practicals that demonstrate some new aspect of theory, pupils should be talked through an introduction to the experiment so they know what it is about, what to look out for, and what is its importance. A worksheet cannot adequately do this. Major developments of scientific theory are also best done with a teacher teaching 'hard'—that is explaining, questioning, demonstrating, turning things this way and that, responding to pupils faces and questions. Worksheets can then be used to either follow up with a sequence of questions, book research, or a further practical, etc. but it is that first synthesis when, hopefully, most of the class will 'get what she's on about'! Likewise, at the end of a section of work, even if pupils have been working at their own pace and have reached different levels of understanding, a class session with the teacher bringing together the concepts. Answering questions, assessing aurally the understanding of the pupils, adds a vital variety and again, an extra interaction that a worksheet cannot provide. (The importance of a teacher teaching is very eloquently described in Joan Solomon's book *Teaching Children in a Laboratory* (6).

5 When to be successful?

Clearly chronic success is not a problem but is the declared aim of some types of worksheet. Practical instructions should lead the pupil to a guaranteed result (providing they are followed properly) and there should be sufficient detail and precision in the instructions to guide all the pupils in the class. Any worksheet that is concerned to develop a practical skill or a study skill (DARTs, etc.) should give the pupil a high rate of success. Simple question and answer sheets, especially if they are to be used as homework or in the lower school, should be largely successful providing that worksheets do not provide the overwhelming majority of the learning material given to the pupils.

Motivation by success need only be a part of a teacher's armoury and motivation by directed improvement can be an equally powerful weapon. American research has shown that getting things wrong is not in itself demotivating and pupils can respond by becoming determined to succeed and get things right if they have their mistakes clearly pointed out and are encouraged to continue (11). If mistakes are not pointed out and being wrong seems to be part of a pupil's intrinsic personal failing that he or she can do nothing about, then naturally a pupil will tend to give up. This throws a great burden on the teacher to mark thoroughly and to go over pupils' work. The great variety of work that has been suggested to complement the use of worksheets would not make a pupil's success certain, never mind chronic.

6 Writing worksheets

Writing worksheets takes a lot of time and expertise. It is always a good idea to look out for published materials that might 'do'. Even with extensive alteration, they will be a considerable saving in time and better presentation. Borrowing materials from other schools either directly or via teachers' centres also saves time.

Aims and objectives of the course and of the worksheet should be itemized so it is clear what is the function of each worksheet. When writing a worksheet the points made in the following checklist should be kept in mind. After the worksheet has been planned, drafted, proof-read, and reproduced it is as well, if it is to be a permanent part of a course, to run a limited edition so that corrections can be made after trialling in the laboratory. It helps every department if a school has a whole-school policy on worksheets and examples are freely available from each department so that departments can have a distinctive style.

'It was found in a number of case-study schools, courses were supplemented by a system of worksheets which all had a similar appearance regardless of the nature of the topic.'   (1)

A checklist for writers of worksheets

Writing
    Syntax is unambiguous and simple
    Punctuation is correct
    Spelling is correct
    Vocabulary can be understood by pupil
    Pleasant tone

Presentation
    Diagrams well drawn
    Layout is clear
    Do not use upper case continuously
    Arouses interest and curiosity
    Is not too similar to many other worksheets
    Legible and well reproduced

Structure
    Clearly laid out and follows on
    Involves a variety of activities
    Leads to an open conclusion wherever possible

Content
   Meets objectives
   Pupils have the basic knowledge it requires

Experiment instruction worksheets
   Safety points emphasized
   Apparatus needs are clear (diagram if necessary)
   Language and vocabulary kept very simple
   Instructions numbered in sequence as a column
   Plenty of space for observations (or use workcard)
   Demands thought on the point of the experiment at beginning
   and end
   Should provide opportunity for writing at length

References

1 Department of Education and Science *Aspects of Secondary Education in England* (HMSO 1979)
2 Beavis R. and Weatherley C. *Worksheets in School Learning* SCET Working Paper 8 1980
3 *Writing in Science: Writing Across Curriculum*; Schools Council (Institute of Education 1975)
4 Department of Education and Science *Language for Life*, Bullock Committee Report (HMSO 1975)
5 Lunzer E. and Gardner K. *The Effective Use of Reading* (Heinemann Educational Books for the Schools Council 1979)
6 Solomon J. *Teaching Children in the Laboratory* (Croom Helm 1980)
7 C. Sutton (ed.) *Communicating in the Classroom* (Hodder and Stoughton 1981)
8 Nuffield Chemistry (Nuffield Foundation for Longman 1967)
9 Harrison C. *Readability in the Classroom* (Cambridge University Press 1980)
10 Association for Science Education *Language in Science* (ASE 1980)
11 Dweck C.S. Learned Helplessness and Negative Evaluation *VCLA Education* Vol 19 No. 2 Winter 1977

6   *Teacher talk*

Introduction

Patterns of talking and listening by pupils will vary enormously depending on the teaching style adopted by the teacher. In laboratories where there is much independent learning by the pupils, talk between pupils and between teacher and individual pupils will predominate. In the teacher-focussed class lesson much more time will be spent in teacher to class talk with the pupils passively listening. HMI found that in 'about one third of the schools visited the dominant teaching style was exposition from the teacher with little or no pupil involvement' (1, 8.12.21). Speech was often limited to factual recall or brief monosyllabic responses. The survey carried out by Lunzer and Gardner (2) shows that pupils in first-year science lessons spend on average 26% of their time listening to their teacher, rising to 31% in fourth-year science lessons (far more time than is spent on practical work). Pupil–pupil discussion occupies under 9% of the time and discussion with the teacher only 4% of the time.

The percentage of pupil's time spent on various activities

	Administrating	Waiting attention	Not involved	Listening	Observing	Practical	Discussing with teacher	Discussing with child	Deliberating	Writing (time sample)	Reading (time sample)	Calculating
First year secondary Science	9	3	8	26	7	23	4	9	1	11	9	1
For all lessons	9	3	10	26	4	14	4	8	3	9	14	4
Fourth year secondary Science	5	0	10	31	8	11	4	7	2	20	10	3
For all lessons	6−	1−	13	29	6	7	3	8	2	17+	15	6

(2, p. 120)

Despite modern trends in science teaching away from the teacher-dominated lesson, it is clear that very many teachers still use the class exposition as their main teaching method. The move towards more pupil-orientated work with pupils learning more independently of the teacher has a long way to go when, on average, only 15% of the time is spent in active discussion by pupils—half the time that is spent on listening.

Teacher talk *can* be immensely exciting and valuable. Even those teachers who are most devoted to pupils learning through independent study should provide demonstrations of complex and conceptually difficult experiments, explanations to the class, introduction and summing up of topics. It gives the class a focus, is interesting, can be exciting, and gives the class a feeling of corporateness. However, the benefits of the extended monologue, the questions to the class, and the 'discussions' between the teacher and a class of 20-30 pupils are now being questioned and could make way for more profitable exchanges between the pupils themselves or a more genuine dialogue between teacher and pupil.

Problems

1 *Teacher exposition*

Teacher exposition to an attentive class of pupils is so commonplace in classrooms and laboratories that is has become over the centuries synonymous with teaching itself. The outsider readily equates the job of teaching with standing in front of a class giving out information. Indeed without an easy access to books or well-equipped laboratories the teacher herself *was* the only educational resource. For most teachers, to hold their classes in rapt attention, to see the dawn of understanding and excitement on their faces, is the great reward in teaching, the pleasure that makes all the hours of preparation and administration worthwhile. Also for many pupils the excitement and sense of things being made clear by a good teacher has made long years spent in school seem profitable and even enjoyable. Pupils are quick to value this and their highest praise is reserved for those teachers whom they can understand and enjoy when they talk to the class. Any method of teaching that always denies teacher and pupils these moments of clarity and mutual enjoyment takes away one of life's most valuable experiences.

There are other more prosaic reasons why teachers spend much of their lessons giving their pupils information—it seems a very quick and efficient method, the teacher knows his or her 'stuff', the pupils do not, and a verbal transmission from teacher to pupil might appear to result in the pupils' learning. Time, the persistent bugbear of education, would seem to favour this quick method, and the pressure of large examination syllabuses means information has to be imparted quickly in order to cover the subject content. The examination pressure also encourages the teacher to keep the information-giving to himself as this information is more accurate and 'scientific'. There is a control over the information (vocabulary, definitions, phrasing) that might be missing if pupils found information from books or each other. This control over information can extend from the scientifically factual to the relationship between science and society. The science teacher can then present even this contentious information in a neutral and balanced fashion. (Nuclear power is often presented as uncontroversial, and the penetrating power of radiation as if it had no human significance.)

Teachers also subconsciously and consciously learn methods of classroom control. Pupils are generally quieter and much less mobile while being talked at and this encourages the teacher to continue to talk rather than allow the pupils to move or to talk themselves. One of the great teaching skills that presents most difficulty to young teachers is how to keep a class quiet so that the teacher can talk. Once learnt this skill is not easily relinquished in favour of the less orderly independence of the pupils.

Pupils also like being talked to, providing they like the teacher and are sufficiently interested. It is easier than finding out for themselves or doing practicals, and their approbation reinforces the teacher in his expository style. (Of course, if the teacher is not stimulating, he will not be liked and many rebellions will make it increasingly difficult for that teacher to continue.)

Science teachers are always faced with the difficulty of scientific concepts and language. In books or in worksheets the teacher may have positively exerted effort to choose a suitable level of language complexity and to have eliminated many of the worst pitfalls for their pupils. Yet in speech, where it appears most easy to be simple and clear, we are at out most convoluted and confusing. In 1969 Douglas Barnes and Harold Rosen analysed the spoken language used in schools. They found that it was very complex, alien to the child's everyday language experience, and could cause pupils grave learning difficulties. (Their book *The Language Learner and the School* (3) has been a major impetus to the move towards independent learning in science as in other subjects.) Barnes and Rosen identified three types of language used in secondary schools:

(a) *Specialist language presented* This includes language forms special to the teacher's subject which he is aware of as a potential barrier to his pupils' understanding, and which he therefore 'presents' to them with *deliberate care.*

(b) *Specialist language not presented* Language forms special to the subject may not be deliberately 'presented' to pupils either (i) because they have previously been introduced, or (ii) because the teacher is unaware that he is using them.

(c) *The language of secondary education* This includes language forms not specific to any school subject, and which pupils would not normally hear or use in speech. (In associating this register of language with secondary education it is not suggested that it cannot be found in some primary school classrooms.)   (3, p. 46)

These forms of language used by the teacher can form a formidable barrier to understanding. Added to this we have the huge problem of scientific vocabulary and prose. This results in many teacher's classroom speech sounding like very old, high-powered science textbooks that the teachers themselves would have rejected for the pupils as being far too difficult. Teacher talk is often laden with concepts—with virtually no opportunity for the pupils to ask for explanations—and for many the required explanations would be needed so frequently that teacher and class would be quite exasperated. Much talk is built on concepts that the pupil may not have fully grasped and as the teacher has now 'gone on' from the original idea, the pupil is left with neither the first nor the second idea within her grasp. Key words and definitions can easily be missed by the pupils through poor attention or because the teacher has not given them enough emphasis. All this can add up to the woeful cry 'I don't understand', which must be one of the greatest causes of pupils disliking science. If one is told something by an expert and one still doesn't understand, the fault often seems to lie within oneself—one fails—and therefore one distances or dislikes the subject.

Apart from the sheer difficulty of the concepts the teacher is trying to get across, there is also the problem of the teacher as an entertainer. If any of us as adults tried to hold the undivided attention of 20-30 of our peers for thirty minutes or more we would feel that we would have to be extremely amusing or very interesting; indeed, not many professional entertainers would attempt the task with talk alone. Teachers can be dull, repetitive, monotonous, tired, and have very irritating voices. (One teacher I knew prepared his lessons and had various OHPs and practical experiments for the pupils but his voice was so grating that even his first few words created great hostility.) Some teachers are not able to explain things clearly. Sometimes teachers have no sense of when to stop, of how to break a lesson into segments so that activities can change and interest be renewed. Non-verbal messages given out by the teacher can reinforce or be counter-productive to what he is saying: anxiety, fear of the class, boredom, etc. can be just as much an influence on a lesson as enthusiasm and excitement. Young teachers often consciously adopt a bright, confident manner that is betrayed by their awkward body movements and high, forced tone of voice. Pupils are usually very aware of the nervousness the teacher is desperately trying to hide.

In an unruly class it is quite impossible to 'teach' the pupils by talking to them. If teacher talk is to be used then the pupils must be quiet enough to hear and to concentrate without distracting noises from their fellow pupils. If only a few are listening, even their interest will soon evaporate. It can be quite distressing to hear a teacher try to explain some complex procedure while breaking every three or four words into 'Johnny, will you please shut up!', 'Sit down!', 'Go outside!'. Absolutely no learning whatsover can take place in such an environment.

The challenge of boisterous pupils is a very obvious one that teachers clearly must learn to master. However, here is also a challenge posed by the very passive class. Pupils sitting quietly *may* be learning something despite a lack of response and if the teacher occasionally asks a question and receives an adequate reply then all appears to be well. Despite this calm, academic atmosphere, I am sure we all remember our own schooldays when we all sat quietly in just such classrooms, dreaming contently while the teacher droned on. Little was learnt and less remembered.

Finally, whatever the composition of the class—mixed-ability or homogeneous—the pace of the teacher will not suit the pace of all members of the class. The clever pupils may well become restless and bored as the obvious is explained, the slow may have lost the thread almost before beginning, and the naughty be looking for more interesting diversions. Clearly the longer the teacher goes on and on the worse this particular problem will become.

2 Teacher-class questions

Teacher-class dialogue is often in the form of the teacher asking questions of selected pupils from the class. Often this is done as a break in a teacher's discourse or to make a point—it is not really done to establish the knowledge gained by the class. Teacher feedback is usually gained through tests and possibly homework and written assignments.

The questions teachers ask members of a class are often closed, requiring factual recall, require only one missing word, or a single 'yes' or 'no'. The questions can also be ambiguous, requiring the pupil to effectively give the answer from facial clues. Teachers often do 'not want improvised reasoning but the name of an object' (3, p. 33). Answers must be given very quickly: the pause for thought allows an embarrassing silence to develop and pupil boredom to begin. This is why teachers often ask pupils to answer who they know will answer quickly. If a slow pupil is asked the lengthening pause can be quickly terminated by a sure-fire-quick-right-answering pupil. Research has also shown that, in general, science teachers prefer to ask boys the questions! (4) Certainly, prolonged answers where the pupil is really exploring his or her own thoughts on the question are usually discouraged. Occasionally pupils may be able to give an extended verbal answer, but this is often not required and the pupil who can give such a competent, quick, exposition is very rare.

There is quite a lot of social aggression in the questioning of a class. Pupils can easily be made to look foolish; their wrong answers held up to ridicule; or at best turned into a cue for a teacher explanation of exactly why it is wrong. This verbal jousting and testing does not encourage pupil talk very much. Even the cleverest can find themselves humiliated publicly, or disliked for being too clever. It is absolutely *not* a suitable method for encouraging concept formation to develop.

Strategies

1 *Teacher exposition*

Looking more or less objectively at our own verbal performance during a lesson can be a very depressing experience and yet it is something that all teachers should do. It is very easy to make a tape of a lesson and then to analyse it very roughly to find out:

(a) who talks during the lesson,
(b) how long each person talks, and
(c) what they are talking about.

Further analysis of recordings can help us to evaluate our own performance as a class teacher. Questions to ask oneself when listening can include the following:

Checklist

Assessing teacher talk

(a) *Audibility* Can all pupils hear what is being said?
Does a pupil who wants to listen, have to strain unduly simply to hear?
Is the teacher's voice too loud for comfort?
Does the teacher insist that *pupil* talk be audible to others?

(b) *Clarity* Is the actual spoken language clear? Do the pupils have difficulty, not in hearing, but in *recognizing* the words they hear?

(c) *Acceptability* Is this teacher talk positively pleasant to listen to?
Are there any features of accent, or indicators of attitude, that lessen the acceptability to pupils of this teacher's talk?
Are there any speech mannerisms which are definitely unfortunate?
(Mannerisms of speech are bound to exist and are not necessarily unhelpful.)
Does the teacher show by his vocabulary, his use of examples, his use of humour, that he understands what pupils are likely to appreciate?

(d) *Variety* Does the teacher realize that his talking can serve many different purposes? (For example: control and discipline; straightforward exposition; stimulus to thought and talk by pupils; clarification and confirmation; relaxation and pleasure.)
Is the type of speech appropriate to the purpose?
Is this speech monotonous or boring?
Is there a helpful variation in pace, pitch, dynamics, tone, and feeling?

(e) *Level* Is the language at an appropriate level for these learners?
Is any of the vocabulary unnecessarily difficult?
Are any of the language structures unnecessarily complex?
When essential new words are introduced is their meaning made clear?

(f) *Interest* Is the subject interesting?
If the subject matter is not very interesting does the teacher try to make it so by introducing analogies, jokes, etc?

(g) *Sense* Does the teacher 'make sense' of the subject?
Is the development of ideas logical? Not fragmented?
Are the important points emphasized?

(h) *Pupil reaction* Are all the pupils listening?
How many are not listening?
Are there any distracting activities/noises?

(i) *Quantity* Whatever the quality of the teacher's speech and use of language, does he talk too much?

(5)

Lesson planning is probably one of the best methods of controlling one's desire to talk too much. If only 2–5 minutes are set aside for an introduction, with other activities such as worksheet, practical, and reading all to be fitted into the lesson, then the impulse towards garrulity can be curbed. It is worth remembering always to ask oneself, 'How long can pupils of 11–14 be reasonably expected to be still, attentive, and quiet?'

2 Teacher-class questions

Teacher The earth spins about an axis. The point at the top about which it spins is called what? What's it called?

Pupil 1 The geographical axis.

Teacher Geographical ...? The point at the top. Almost right. Yes David?

Pupil 2 North

Teacher Yes, north. And the point at which the magnet appears to be—at the top there, just underneath the ground—what's the name of that point there?

Pupil 3 Magnetic north

Teacher Magnetic north. If I was standing on the top of the magnetic north with a compass, what would it do?

Pupil 4 It would go round and round and round

Teacher It wouldn't point in any direction at all. Supposing if I was standing at the geographic north, what would it do there?

Pupil 5 Point to the magnetic north

Teacher Right, what was the name of this angle between the magnetic and the geographical north? Yes, Gary?

Pupil 6 Angle of declination

Teacher Angle of declination. Right, here's a difficult one. Now, I've put a spot there—that's supposed to represent the magnetic north—and the geographic north is the point at which it spins round about. Now if I come down that line there to a point there, can anyone tell me what the angle of declination is going to be? Yes, Bill?

Pupil 7 Nought

Teacher   Nought. Yes. There's no angle between the magnetic north and the geographical north. They're both on the same line.

(6, p. 28)

The above transcript is a classic example of a teacher asking questions in a class. Seven pupils answer in, on average, three words each; only factual recall is required; the questions are ambiguous.

Before asking a class questions it is as well to ask oneself, 'Why am I asking these questions?' There are many situations when a teacher can constructively ask questions of a class as a whole. On a mundane level, questions can provide a quick and amusing method of testing simple factual information (such as symbols and valencies of elements).

A class may be brought together at the beginning of a lesson to be reminded by questioning of the subject of the last lesson, or of information the pupils have that will set the scene for the forthcoming lesson. Closed questions requiring simple recall and more open-ended questions can be used. Carefully structured questioning by the teacher can lead a class through a series of closed questions to a new conceptual discovery. However, one of the most valuable uses of teacher questions is to give the class, as equals with their teacher, the chance to explore new or complicated ideas. Communal exploration with class and teacher together can be a wonderful, if rare, experience. Time is needed for this, with pupils being given time and a warm atmosphere so that they can talk freely—the class must also be willing to let its members talk at length and provide support—a very hard condition to meet. The teacher must not dominate or rework all that pupils say. It is, I feel, very easy to become complacent. I imagine the teacher in the above transcript may well have felt that this interchange was a warm, communal exploration towards concept formation which it clearly is not.

HMI found that

'It was through skilful questioning that teachers succeeded in generating thoughtful responses from their classes.' 'How?' and 'Why?' questions, and those which 'called for some re-working of information' were especially productive, as was readiness on the part of the teacher 'to show interest in the processes of thought that might lead to the pupils' arriving at a partly or wholly untenable conclusion.'   (1, 6, 4.12)

It is very easy to ask only recall or yes/no questions, and even 'pseudoquestions' where the question appears to need an open answer but the dissatisfaction shown by the teacher indicates that really only a fact or a name was required. If pupils are to respond in an extended manner then the class must be sufficiently interested and controlled to cope with this.

A very common but less valuable use of questions is as an attention-arousing break in teacher talk, often aimed at restless pupils. It is very reasonable to ask questions of individuals who do not appear to be listening—this is an excellent form of classroom control—but again if many of the class are clearly 'far away' then the value of one's talk is being lost and should be abandoned. However, if the teachers talk is not too long there is a case for the teacher questioning the class and for allowing pupils to question the teacher. Questions are often misguidedly used to provide feedback to the teacher on how much the class, as a whole, has understood, from a class on whether the topic has been understood is not easy to guage from the answers to questions—faces will show much more. It is only too easy to give ourselves a false sense of security by asking bright pupils questions—both teacher and pupil can be partners in mutual self-satisfaction, or pupils may be encouraged to hide their uncertainties and give an acceptable answer to avoid humiliation. Questions from the teacher stand a much greater chance of being effective feedback or learning experiences when asked to groups or individuals as the teacher moves round the class. Answers can take time, and most valuable of all, can be followed up so that the understanding (or misunderstanding) is probed and becomes clear.

Teachers must also be careful which pupils answer their questions and how often. Quite subconsciously many teachers question the boys, rather than the girls. This is partly because teachers have higher expectations of boys' abilities (especially in science subjects) and partly because boys are more extrovert in their behaviour and demand that questions be asked to them   (7, p. 280). Some pupils will irritate us by the length and untidiness of their answers. I usually try to have a pattern of asking questions so that I ask all pupils on benches 1, 3, 2, 4 in order so that all pupils do get a chance, but my plan is not so obvious that they can easily predict who will be the next victim. Sometimes for mechanical questions (symbols, valencies, answers to exercises) I do go in a very obvious order so the answers are ready.

It might well be said that the pupils' response to their teacher's questions is largely governed by the teacher's response to their answers.

'In responding to the pupils' answers to questions, the teacher should try, as far as it is felt possible, *to accept an explanation in the pupil's own terms*. If this is not done, pupils will be very much less willing to respond openly and will end up making scientific noises, rather than trying to express the understanding towards which they are groping.' (8, p. 15)

HMI also commented on how teachers could respond to pupils answers in a way that would help their confidence and not deny it.

'The best teachers were sensitive to differences in language, and led their pupils discreetly and by a variety of means towards a wider range of language use, and a surer command of language itself.' (1, 6, 4.17)

Answers of one word of 'yes' or 'no' should be explained or extended so that the pupil does have to think. Care is needed over the teacher's own clues to the answer—the frown as the wrong answer begins and the smile and 'Good' as the right answer is given. Although the smile and quick 'Good' are rewards they may not allow the pupil to explore verbally in the future for fear of the frown, or he may feel only a quick answer will receive the smile. Above all pupils should be allowed time to think before replying.

References

1 Department of Education and Science *Aspects of Secondary Education in England* (HMSO 1979)
2 Lunzer E. and Gardner, K. *The Effective Use of Reading* (Heinemann Educational Books for the Schools Council 1979)
3 Barnes D., Britten J., and Rosen H. *Language, the Learner and the School* (Penguin 1969)
4 Serbin L. 'Girls & Maths' and Dweck C. and Licht B. 'Sex Differences in Achievement Orientations: Consequences for academic choices and attainments' in Marland M. (ed) *Sexual Differentiation and Schooling* (Heinemann Educational Books 1983)
5 Hughes J. A. R. *Language in Chemistry* Unit 2 (Scottish Curriculum Development Service Memorandum 43, 1980)
6 Association for Science Education *Language in Science* (ASE 1980)
7 Kelly A. *The Missing Half* (Manchester University Press 1981)
8 Prestt B. (ed.) *Language in Science* (ASE 1980)

7 Talking and listening by pupils

Introduction

Pupil talk in a lesson has many functions. It increases the understanding of concepts, enables pupils to learn how to communicate clearly with others, makes them active learners, gives them a diversity of viewpoints and a critical tolerance of others' ideas.

The most important reason for encouraging pupil talk is that it will increase the pupils' understanding of scientific concepts. Concepts are embodied in language, even in our thoughts. Our ideas are built up of words and phrases that make sense to us; other people's words and phrases may be remembered, but rarely, and it is our own reworking and collecting together of words and examples that help us define and therefore understand concepts. This exploration and collection can be done in our heads. Very advanced students will do this very frequently when they have to plan and write essays and assignments, but for most pupils most of the time this exploration *will be done only through talk*. If we do not provide the opportunity for our pupils to talk through concepts then the chances of them thinking them through at all, never mind successfully, is remote. This function of exploratory talk has been very clearly stated by Michael Marland:

'The way into ideas, the way of making ideas truly one's own is to be able to think them through, and the best way to do this for most people is to talk them through. Thus talking is not merely a way of conveying existing ideas to others; it is also a way by which we explore ideas, clarify them, and make them our own. Talking things over allows the sorting of ideas, and gives rapid and extensive practice towards the handling of ideas.'

(1, p. 125)

Scientific concepts are often extremely complicated; their meaning can vary depending on the context (nucleus in an atom, a cell); many are abstract and cannot be seen or perceived; relationships between concepts are very hard to define (element, compound, molecule); some concepts appear to defy our everyday experiences (work, energy, power). The process of truly understanding scientific concepts is very slow. Osborne and Gilbert have studied how pupils grow to understand concepts (or do not succeed) and they see the building up of this understanding as the collecting together of past experiences, instances, of defining characteristics, also of non-instances and non-attributes (2). Teacher talk can give some instances and attributes, but not nearly as many as would be found in an exploratory discussion amongst those groping towards an understanding. The teacher talk may actually bypass all or most of the pupil's experiences and thus be quite redundant. Discussions amongst pupils is a pooling of facts and experiences and can actually speed up the process of concept formation as well as making the understanding deeper.

One of the main aims of science education is to give our pupils the ability to reason and to be able to communicate verbally with others. Passive listening to a teacher will not help our pupils to argue a case, to listen actively to their peers, and to refute or accept the arguments of others. When one listens to pupils (or indeed adults) much of the speech is implied, sentences are left unfinished or completed by the listener. Science education is about precision and this applies almost more to pupils' *communication* (verbal and written) than to their measuring and practical skills. Discussions and arguments between pupils will make the participants much more explicit—if the meaning is not clear they will have to go on to explain it to the others.

Whereas much pupil talk in a teacher-focussed lesson is reduced to one or two words addressed to the teacher—or to social chatter behind her back—pupil discussion can result in pupils extending

Length of utterance		*Group 1*	*Group 2*	*Group 3*	*Group 4*
Holophrastic	Single words, grunts, etc.	13%	11	8	10
Telegraphic	Incomplete phrases	19%	28	21	24
Holistic	A complete phrase— sentence	63%	57	64	63
Discourse	More than one sentence, linked in meaningful way.	5%	4	7	3

(3, p. 19)

their talk into using whole sentences much more frequently. John Horsfield in his study of pupil-controlled groups (3) found after studying his discussion groups that most of the contributions were in whole sentences.

By comparison researchers from the Scottish Curriculum Development Service following Tommy, a pupil in a Scottish secondary school, found that during one day

'I Only in one context (car craft) did Tommy really engage a teacher in oral language and move towards exploratory talk/opinion.

II In one class Tommy was mute, in one class he answered one question and in another three questions. In none of these cases did Tommy form a sentence; the answers were all abbreviated and offered certainties not doubts.

III Most lesson time was taken up with teacher talk.' (4)

Active listening—as in conversations when the pupil will expect to respond to what is being said—and talking both increase the pupils participation in his or her own learning and decrease boredom and frustration. Teachers often try to break their monologues with questions to the class, but few individuals have the opportunity to answer and that answer may only be one word!

As scientists we want our pupils to be able to distinguish between what is accepted 'common sense' and fact. This cannot be done by merely accepting 'expert' (i.e. the teacher's) opinion but has to be done through a dialectic process. In many new science courses (*Siscon* or *Science in Society*) the discussion of opinions and the social aspects of science are the basis of the course. Discussion by pupils is clearly acknowledged as one of the main methods of working.

Only by talking and participating in discussion can a pupil develop into an articulate, thoughtful adult, and to achieve this must be one of the most important general aims of education.

Within science teaching there are two ways of teaching pupils: to give them the information, or to let them find out for themselves. Whatever means is used by the teacher (and both will be appropriate at different times) the Bullock Committee have emphasized the necessity of pupil talk:

'Nothing has done more to confuse current educational debate than the simplistic notion that 'being told' is the polar opposite of 'finding out for oneself'. In order to accept what is offered when we are told something, we have to have somewhere to put it: and having somewhere to put it means that the framework of past knowledge and experience into which it must fit is adequate as a means of interpreting and apprehending it. Something approximating to 'finding out for ourselves' needs therefore to take place if we are to be successfully told. The development of this individual context for a new piece of information, the forging of the links that give it meaning, is a task that we customarily tackle by talking to other people.' (5, para. 4.9, p. 50)

Problems

There are many forms of discussion possible within a science lesson. However, for the purpose of this chapter I am using the term discussion to mean discussion between small groups of pupils on a pre-arranged topic. Discussions between a teacher and a class of twenty or more pupils are not, in my view, true discussions. Discussions during practicals most certainly do occur and are very valuable. However, they are usually self-generating, revolve round the practical task, and do not require any deeper analysis or refinement. The special problems of groups of pupils and a teacher holding discussions are mentioned later.

1 *Pupil discussion*

The greatest problem presented by small groups of pupils talking together is that of maintaining control over the group, the topic they are to discuss, and over the whole laboratory. Teachers are worried that pupils when encouraged to talk will quickly turn to TV, football, gossip—and not the 'pre-arranged topic'. The sheer volume of noise as four or five groups discuss a topic animatedly may also alarm many teachers, who would be afraid of their colleagues' reactions to this hubbub. Other teachers might also dislike the delegation of classroom control to the pupils and feel that they were not 'in charge'. Others might feel uncomfortably redundant. Another problem that arises in all lessons and all forms of teaching, is that of coping with the attention-seeking pupil, and some teachers fear that in a small group these pupils may dominate to the severe detriment of others' learning.

Many of these problems can be overcome by the teacher clearly pinpointing the purpose of the discussion and a careful selection of the task. The purpose and the task will then influence the group size and its composition. Teachers' knowledge of their pupils will also influence how they select groups.

A constant theme when looking at language and science is the science teachers' regard for scientific accuracy and precision as expressed in scientific vocabulary and prose. In pupil discussions there will be almost no control over these aspects of science, and yet perhaps this freedom will bring the greatest benefit to the pupils. Gilbert and Osborne (2) have emphasized that it is only by putting ideas to the test of past experience and of accreting examples that thoughts can develop. Talking about things outside school, jokes, and digressions may be a quicker and sounder way forward than the traditional memorized definition so mellifluous to teacher's ears. When Gilbert and Osborne interviewed science pupils they found that it was very rare for students who had memorized a number of formal, scientific definitions to display any real understanding of how to relate or apply these to instances.

Practical difficulties abound. When would be a good time to split the class into discussion groups? In a mixed-ability class where pupils may be doing many different tasks and be at different levels this can be a very awkward decision.

Teachers are often frightened of what will happen when the groups have been safely settled, the topic broached, and then pupils talk irrelevantly, or begin to quarrel, or there are no ideas forthcoming, or worst of all, there is an uneasy, embarrassed silence. More than all other reasons I feel that it is the teacher's fear of the embarrassing silent failure that prevents many from using pupil discussion groups in their lessons, and yet this can be quite simply avoided. D. Barnes and F. Todd, who have done major research into pupils' communication and learning in small groups, emphasized that the teachers' reactions on hearing tapes of their pupils' discussions were commonly of surprise and delight. They were surprised because the quality of the children's discussions typically far exceeded the calibre of their contributions in class; and were pleased to hear the children manifesting unexpected skills and competences (6, p. ix).

Teacher-led discussions are an obvious way of overcoming some of the problems of control—especially over the topic to be discussed and the scientific validity of the ideas. However, there are as many disadvantages as advantages associated with the teacher being present.

Firstly:

'It is possible for teachers to develop strategies for participating without dominating but these techniques are at their hardest in subjects with few periods and much explaining—such as science.' (1, p. 134)

Teachers also will tend to dominate the discussion and be a focus for their pupils who will seek acceptance and praise from the teacher. It is only too easy for the teacher to inhibit the exploratory pupil talk that the discussion was devised to encourage. This inhibition can take many forms—even when done by the most sensitive and caring teacher, as can be seen in these comments.

Some hypotheses about teacher-led discussions
(after Adelmann, Elliott *et al.*)

1 Asking many questions of pupils ... may raise too many of the teacher's own ideas and leave no room for those of the pupil. Responding to pupils' questions with many ideas may stifle the expression of their own ideas.
2 Re-formulating problems in the teacher's own words may prevent pupils from clarifying them for themselves.
3 When the teacher changes the direction of enquiry or point of discussion, pupils may fail to contribute their own ideas. They will interpret such actions as attempts to get them to conform with his own line of reasoning.
4 When the teacher always asks a question following a pupil's response to his previous question, he may prevent pupils from introducing their own ideas.
5 When the teacher responds to pupils' ideas with utterances like 'good', 'yes', 'right' , 'interesting', etc., he may prevent others from expressing alternative ideas. Such utterances may be interpreted as rewards for providing the responses required by the teacher. (7, p. 63)

Teachers may wish to use pupil discussion as a means of getting feedback from their pupils. This also has its dangers—the pupil may become quite embarrassed, and may try not to reveal their lack of understanding, whereas in a teacherless group they might be much more open about their learning difficulties.

In a science course there has to be a balance between the teacher exposition which can be very exciting, stimulating, and illuminating (not an endless monologue) and pupils talk amongst themselves where they can explore and develop their ideas without the constraint of the teacher's criticism or approbation. However good the teacher's exposition, without pupil talk the understanding gained may be very short-lived.

2 *Listening*

'Listening' is a word we use to cover very different activities. Listening can mean: a state of quiescence that is almost akin to a doze, it can mean the reception of words by the listener with mute acceptance, or it can mean an active intellectual state when the words heard stimulate a bringing together of new and old information, a questioning and the desire to respond. Listening can only be a way towards learning if it is *active* and the pupils are thinking while listening. When this happens it is a most stimulating and successful form of learning—but it is not to be mistaken for the passive doze.

'Pupils who spend so much of their time listening may need more opportunities than they are given to confirm their understanding and to relate it to other experience.' (8, p. 95)

Irrespective of the oratorical gifts of the teacher there are great differences in the way whole classes will respond. In my experience in inner city schools teachers can have difficulty in getting their pupils to listen at all whereas in some country schools pupils may be much more passive and even difficult to stimulate (5). It is a great skill with turbulent classes to get the pupils to sit quietly, to ignore minor distractions, and not to interrupt irrelevantly. Once that has been achieved, however, the pupils will then listen actively (sometimes too much so!).

One of the aims of education is to encourage in pupils the ability and the confidence to criticize and evaluate information, verbal as well as written. Much of the information that comes to adults is verbal via TV, films, and radio, and our pupils must be able to recognize bias, tones of voice, the value, depth, logic, and inconsistencies in such information. Passive unquestioning listening to an 'expert' (the teacher) will not encourage these skills to grow.

Adults not only have to respond to information internally by thinking but will frequently be asked to respond verbally, as when we have to argue a case or even hold conversations. Here, accurate listening to the other person, selection of important points, remembering, and formulating an appropriate answer all have to be done very quickly. This cannot all be done in drama and special English language lessons.

If teachers talk too much, then pupils are also having to listen too long and too passively. Therefore it is very important that pupils should also listen to people other than their teacher, and as this usually happens during conversations, discussion, and arguments, they will have to listen actively.

Strategies

1 *Pupil discussion*

(a) Creating a climate for discussion
The attitude of the teacher to pupils' discussion is vitally important—pupils must be able to see that their talk is valued by the

teacher. Self-control on the part of the pupils and warmth towards and from the teacher mean that there will be a relaxed, friendly atmosphere in which discussion can flourish and the teacher will rarely have to exert her hierarchical authority.

Not only the psychological but also the physical conditions should be conducive to civilized discussion. Pupils often talk in a much more mature way in the environment of the library which is often carpeted with easy chairs rather than stark, messy, general class-rooms. Laboratories *can* be quite good places for discussion, especially if there are tables rather than benches. Groups should, as much as is possible, be arranged round tables rather than in lines along a bench. The quieter the general atmosphere the better (e.g. it is not a good moment to have technicians clear up).

Classes that have not been used to discussions in science should have the opportunity to talk about this new experience beforehand. It should be explained how discussions can be helpful to them, as discussions can

(a) help to bring together existing knowledge and new experience,
(b) provide the opportunity to formulate one's own understanding,
(c) involve taking on other people's ideas as well as the new know-ledge and information,
(d) involve building a common construct, which is more powerful than anything one individual might build (9, p. 46),
(e) be a preparation for adult life, and not just be of benefit to their science education. The teacher's expectations of the group's be-haviour should be explained.

Pupils are always distrustful of new experiences and do like to be forewarned and given the confidence to undertake a new venture.

Classes vary enormously; with some classes this form of learning could only be started after the group had been very gently led towards self-confidence in speech, in some classes such freedom would only be abused until pupils had been trained into self-discipline. However, to abandon the idea of ever running small-group discussions with a particular class is a very real confes-sion of teacher failure.

(b) Knowledge acquired beforehand by the pupils

'Nobody likes to be wrong, especially in front of rivals or superiors, so the pupils' sense of competence, their sense of having something relevant to contribute, will go far to determine the morale with which they approach the task, and the patience with which they continue to work together at it.'   (6, p. 81)

Barnes and Todd found in their study on *Communication and Learning in Small Groups* (quoted above) that the success of many of the groups was partly due to a preliminary presentation of the topic to the whole class. Pupils could see some of the likely approaches and found some of the suggestions valuable. Materials relevant to the discussion were also helpful, such as a text, and apparatus was especially useful.

Many useful discussions in science can centre round TV programmes—providing all members have seen the programme—or on scientific issues with importance for society, where all pupils can air their opinions. Some of the most effective discussions involve pupils bringing their own everyday experiences and common sense to bear on a problem.

(c) The task

The task set should be appropriate to the current subject matter. Pupils will often react against an artificial situation. The task set should have a clearly defined end-product which is within the capabilities of the group. At first the tasks should be closed, for example classifying objects or sequencing information. As discussion becomes easier the tasks can become more open-ended. Initially, the time set aside for discussion should be quite short and then extended later as expertise develops. Pupils should know how much time is available for discussion. Different types of discussion are susceptible to different amounts of structuring by the teacher. If the purpose of the discussion is to allow very free-ranging talk with the emphasis on exploration then little structure will be required. Pupils will need to be told very clearly that exploration is the purpose of their discussion as they may very easily imagine that somewhere there lies the 'right idea' that they must find! Little structure is only possible if pupils have a lot of knowledge so that they are not continually frustrated by their own lack of information. If the teacher does not want to guide her pupils towards general conclusions or specific end products then some structure is helpful. However, this should not be too rigid as the group's thoughts may well not follow the same pattern as the teacher's and the questions may confuse rather than guide.

Here is an example of a general sequence that could be used for discussions following practical work:

Reporting   What did you see? Did you see the same? etc.
Interpretation   How do you account for that? Why do you describe it like that? Why is your observation different from his? etc.

Application   Does this remind you of anything else? Can you find other cases like this? What will happen if ...? etc.

Here are two examples of very different tasks, one closed and one quite open (from Barnes and Todd):

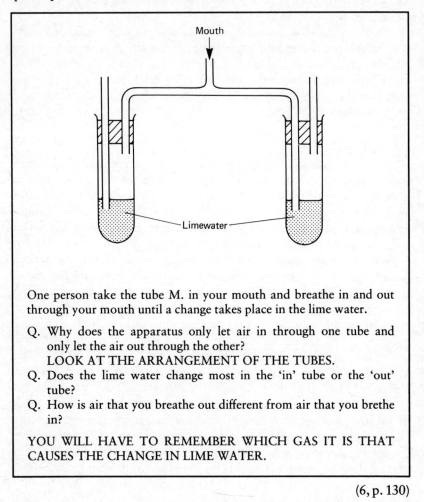

One person take the tube M. in your mouth and breathe in and out through your mouth until a change takes place in the lime water.

Q. Why does the apparatus only let air in through one tube and only let the air out through the other?
   LOOK AT THE ARRANGEMENT OF THE TUBES.
Q. Does the lime water change most in the 'in' tube or the 'out' tube?
Q. How is air that you breathe out different from air that you brethe in?

YOU WILL HAVE TO REMEMBER WHICH GAS IT IS THAT CAUSES THE CHANGE IN LIME WATER.

(6, p. 130)

WORK/ENERGY
We use the idea of WORK as a measure of how much ENERGY changes from one form to another.
WORK is done when a force moves.
Here are some energy changes. Discuss them, and work out the ones in which work is done:
(a) Electricity to light in a light bulb
(b) Heat to movement in a steam engine
(c) Food to movement on a bicycle
Think of any other energy changes.
Is work always done when energy changes form?

(6, p. 129)

Barnes and Todd concluded 'that there is much to be said for ending even the tightest task with an open invitation to discuss other related issues which occur to pupils' (6, p. 84).

Many of the language-orientated tasks discussed earlier in this book provide excellent starting points for discussion: the DART activities, marking work, notes, worksheets, and, of course, practical work itself.

Other ideas have been collected by the Language in Chemistry team.

Ideas for starting purposeful talk
1 *Marking other people's work.* After a piece of work, e.g. writing a report, writing about an experiment, groups can be asked to assess each others' work and to discuss the reasons for their decisions.
2 *Write a story/script.* Groups are asked to discuss and then to prepare a science fiction story/TV script, e.g. space explorers landing on a planet which has an atmosphere of nitrogen and hydrogen. The story could possibly be recorded.
3 *Project.* Each group can be given a different task in relation to a particular topic, and asked to present their conclusions to the other groups. The presentations would be the result of a group discussion and could take a variety of forms, e.g. oral, written, recorded, slides, OHP transparencies.
4 *Definitions.* Having studied the atomic nature of matter, groups of pupils could be asked to consider the difference between the terms element, compound and mixture. They could be provided with poppet beads, centicubes etc., asked to produce models and describe them in writing. Final descriptions could be the result of group discussions.
5 *Finding the thread of the argument.* Divide some written material into parts and shuffle them so that they do not follow the correct sequence.

Pupils have to discuss the situation and try to work out a logical sequence (DART).

6 *Devising questions.* Each discussion group could devise one set of questions on a current topic. These can be exchanged with another group who attempt to answer the questions.

7 *Make up a tape-slide sequence.* Each group could be asked to prepare a short tape-slide sequence on a suitable topic, e.g. how soap is made. Where slides or OHP transparencies are available a commentary could be prepared. It is useful to tell the pupils what the audience is to be.

8 *Selection.* A group of pupils can be asked to look at a set of photographs, slides or passages of writing and, as a result of discussion, select a few to illustrate a teaching point.

9 *Making a chart.* As a result of group-discussion, groups of pupils could prepare charts to present certain facts or processes. (4)

Other ideas might include classification tasks, comparing and contrasting (different groups of elements, animals, or plants), devising experiments, drafting sets of rules or collecting examples.

There is some controversy over the wisdom of always asking pupils to write after they have finished their discussions (6, p. 85). Pupils on the one hand may see talk as a mere preliminary to the writing and therefore avoid much explanatory discussion. However, making private notes on the discussion helps pupils to summarize and clarify the discussion itself. Some discussions will have written products as their goal.

(d) Composition of the groups

Small group discussion really does mean small group—with two being a minimum and four pupils a maximum, so that all pupils will take an active role.

If groups become larger than two or three then there is an increasing likelihood that one or more pupils will become distanced and silent. The fewer the numbers involved the more time and pressure each participant will have to speak. Although the social aspects of small group work are important, with larger groups a very strong social interaction, with people playing out roles within the group, might seriously interfere with learning. Different discussion tasks might require larger numbers of pupils, such as the coordination of complicated projects or the comparison of different experimental results. If apparatus and materials are short the teacher may have to have larger groups, although this should be avoided wherever possible.

There is a very great divergence of philosophy and practice on whether groups of pupils should be allowed to be in friendship groups or in teacher-allocated groups. Initially, when pupils are not used to small group work, the social pressures and the feeling of being 'exposed' will be at its greatest. Under these circumstances it is more comfortable for the pupils to select their own groups. However there are very real disadvantages inherent in self-selected groups: friendship groups may frequently not provide the right mixture of differing attitudes and viewpoints, and between close friends their normal intimacy might act as a barrier to more exploratory scientific talk and might lead to a following of the other, or to embarrassment, or to chatter.

As pupils become more used to discussion work the teacher can start to manipulate the composition of the groups. For tasks whose purpose is largely exploration then self-selected, single sex groups might be appropriate, but when pupils have confidence in their discussion and the teacher wants them to argue and justify, then mixed-sex teacher-selected groups would be more appropriate (6, p. 87).

In general, experienced groups should include pupils of different viewpoints, ideas, and development but not be too widely spread in terms of ability. Another factor in allocating pupils to groups is the personality of each pupil. Shy pupils will not contribute if they are in a very noisy group, pupils with bad behaviour should not be grouped together. One factor that teachers must control is the grouping of the dominant pupils.

'Often, if not always, what is done in and by a group is largely determined by the strongest personality in that group. The wise teacher will bear this in mind when allocating and reallocating pupils to groups. (The strongest personality is not always the ablest pupil.)' (10, p. 192)

A pupil who is overbearing and dominant in a group must be taken aside and have this pointed out. (The series of cartoons on pages 128–9 illustrates many of the pitfalls participants can fall into— perhaps this could be used to point the errors of their ways.) If a pupil continues to spoil the discussion of the rest of the group they can be moved to another group. If this fails they must be removed from discussion group work. Teachers take immense pains to control the learning environment of their pupils—friendship groups can turn into 'the prison of the peer group' (Michael Marland) and undo much of the good that the teacher has meticulously planned.

It is sometimes suggested that pupils should appoint a 'chairperson' within a group, but Barnes and Todd (6, p. 85) found that pupils 'did not find it easy to chair a group tactfully, nor to accept

Discussion Techniques

When you are taking part in a discussion remember the following points. They are *very* important.

1 Remember you are taking part in a discussion
(a) to learn
(b) to help other people to learn.

2 Always have a paper and pencil handy during discussions.

3 Ask for anything you do not understand to be explained.

4 If two people have misunderstood each other, help them out.

5 If someone has said something which you think is important, remind the group about it.

6 Always let other people 'have their say', even if you are bursting to say something.

7 Be prepared to change your mind if you have been proved wrong.

8 Do not shout people down just because you don't agree with them.

9 Do not show off in a discussion.

10 You must take part in a discussion even if you feel shy.

11 Listen carefully to what everyone else in the group says.

12 Always have one member of the group writing down the most important points discussed and any decisions that the group has made.

the guidance of a chairman of their own age'. Their suggestion is to build in some of these functions into the task itself, for example:

1 After you've been talking for about five minutes ask yourselves: 'How far have we got? Are we on the point or have we been sidetracked? What line should we follow up next?' (Don't spend more than about two minutes on this, though.)
2 At the end of the talk allow yourselves several minutes to decide together what have been the main points of your discussion and the arguments that have been put forward.
3 Write down in note form a brief summary of the discussion. Keep these notes for yourself as a record of what was said. (6, p. 85)

(e) Monitoring learning through discussion

While small-group discussions are going on in the classroom or the laboratory the teacher will doubtless be roving from group to group—joining in, gently directing when appropriate. However well-intentioned these incursions may be they will not be very helpful in terms of monitoring the learning as the presence of the teacher is likely to have quite an effect on the group. Notes written up at the end of discussions are likely to be either for very personal use or quite a finished group product, neither of which will reflect the variety of experiences undergone during discussion. The best way of monitoring talk is to tape record it and to record the same groups discussing different topics. Barnes and Todd outline six reasons for a teacher to tape pupils' talk.

1 To find if pupils have understood and can apply essential principles.
2 To find out how pupils reach conclusions.
3 To see if tasks are suited to pupils.
4 To monitor social interactions.
5 To gain insights into pupil's strengths as well as weaknesses.
6 To monitor her own intervention in the work of groups. (6, pp. 89–90)

Pupils are becoming increasingly used to the presence of tape recorders. However it is a good idea to let pupils tape themselves and the teacher before the discussion begins and to play it back so they hear their own voices. Most will be familiar with the workings of a cassette player. Useful discussions on discussions can be held when the recording is played back! This clearly helps pupils discussion skills.

A final word of encouragement on the subject of pupil discussions from the ASE:

'Small group discussions need to be open, tentative, exploring, warm, flexible—and not closed with some bold assertions and acceptance or rejection. This is a difficult form of class-management to learn, but when one considers the huge amount of time and resources spent on the very difficult management of practical work it does not look too daunting.' (9)

2 *Listening*

Discussions between pupils and between a pupil and a teacher help the development of most of the active listening skills; pupils have to listen attentively, note mentally what is being said, relate it to other facts and ideas, assess it for bias and consistency, and formulate a response. Many of the discussion tasks set by the teacher will require the pupils to criticize or evaluate information, will require them to form hypotheses together, to speculate, and to argue.

Teachers have always tried to encourage their pupils to listen to their teachers more carefully! Many of the strategies outlined in the first two sections on teacher exposition and teacher–class questions should help considerably to increase active listening, even if it means that pupils actually listen for less time. If the teacher is interesting and brief then the pupils will pay more attention to what he or she says. Likewise, if questions require thoughtful answers rather than stock responses, the pupils are more likely to listen.

Other strategies can be used specifically to develop listening. Pupils can be asked to make their own notes from the teacher's explanation or from films or tapes that they have seen and heard. In many ways this is rather a difficult exercise to set as it requires extremely advanced note-making skills and unless these are adequate much information will be lost in worrying about the notes rather than the content of the talk. Once pupils are adequate note-makers (they can select information, organize it, and then note it down) they can be asked to make notes from short films or tapes that have been preselected for the simplicity and clearness of their points. This can be repeated with slightly more complex films and tapes. It is much harder to take aural notes than notes from a text where one can interrogate, go back and forward, quote and the information is always accessible. Only at sixth-form level will pupils be able to take notes from a mini-lecture. In the sixth form this skill will have to be developed in those pupils who go on to higher education.

The main avenues to develop listening skills lie through pupil–pupil and pupil–teacher discussion with the responsibility lying with the teacher to make her own talk to the class sufficiently interesting and brief to be listened to actively.

Appendix

Practical notes

To study small group discussions you would have to bear the following points in mind:

1　The influence of your own attitudes to pupil talk: how can you communicate to the pupils that you think their talk is worthwhile?
2　Pupils' grasp of the subject matter:
　(i)　Content of the task—familiar or strange? Will pupils be using everyday knowledge or new conceptual structures?
　(ii)　Written or pictorial or filmed material?
　(iii)　Apparatus to be manipulated?
3　How the task is presented:
　(i)　'Tight' or 'loose' structure?
　(ii)　Emphasis on getting to a 'correct' answer or on the quality of the discussion?
　(iii)　Must a solution be agreed on and presented in writing? Can there be only one solution?
　(iv)　Is descriptive observation and action called for, or the generation of rationally argued explanations?
　(v)　Whether to use an agenda, or to instruct the children to recap and summarise and to share chairman-like functions?
　(vi)　Invitation to discuss new but related issues?
4　Composition of the groups:
　(i)　Size and sex of group?
　(ii)　Should members choose one another?
5　Equipment:
　(i)　Tape or cassette?
　(ii)　Trying to ensure good quality sound
　(iii)　Recording in separate room?
6　How to minimise recorder shyness:
　(i)　Allowing children time to get used to their own recorded voices
　(ii)　Teacher making sure his/her own voice is recorded too
　(iii)　Encouraging expression of children's reaction to the sound of their own voices
　(iv)　Giving children some control over the tape recorder
　(v)　Allowing them to replay their own discussion
7　Listening to the recordings:
　(i)　Alone or with an informal working group?
　(ii)　Repeated listening—sorting out what is happening
　(iii)　Decisions about what you are looking for:
　　(a)　talk that is significant for learning
　　(b)　'presenting' versus 'sharing'
　　(c)　pupils joining in construction of lines of thought. Cognitive strategies?

(d) how social relations are organized and managed

(e) the effects of your own participation

(iv) Identification of significant episodes that exemplify (a)–(e) above. What features are you using as evidence? Are your interpretations of these features shared by other teachers in your work group?

(v) Listening to the recording along with the children. Do they share your judgments and interpretations of what was said?   (6, p. 94–5)

References

1 Marland M. *Language Across the Curriculum* (Heinemann Educational Books 1977)
2 Osborne R.J. and Gilbert J.K. *An Approach to Student Understanding of Basic Concepts in Science* (Institute of Educational Technology, University of Surrey 1979)
3 Horsfield J. *Pupil-controlled Groups* Occasional Paper (University of Leicester School of Education 1978)
4 Hughes J.A.R. *Language in Chemistry* Unit 2 (Scottish Curriculum Development Service, Memorandum 43, 1980)
5 Department of Education and Science *Language for Life* Bullock Committee Report (HMSO 1975)
6 Barnes D. and Todd F. *Communicating and Learning in Small Groups* (Routledge and Kegan Paul 1977)
7 Sutton C. (ed.) *Communicating in the Classroom* (Hodder and Stoughton 1981)
8 Department of Education and Science *Aspects of Secondary Education in England* (HMSO 1979)
9 Association for Science Education *Language in Science* (ASE 1980)
10 Lunzer E. and Gardner K. *The Effective Use of Reading* (Heinemann Educational Books for the Schools Council 1979)

8 Information skills

Introduction

Information skills include all the skills needed to find information in libraries and books, the two most vital sources of information, and also finding information from non-book sources such as TV, slides, tapes, radio programmes, and the environment outside school. Some schools have really tried to tackle information skills in its widest meaning (as in the INSCRU Information Skills in the Curriculum Research Unit in London schools (1)), but in this chapter I am really concerned with written material as found in libraries, books, periodicals, and cuttings. Also discussed in this chapter is the use of information skills in writing longer essays or projects, as it is in these assignments that the need for a high degree of competence in this skills is most acute. The divisions between groups of skills are arbitrary and information skills cannot easily be divorced from advanced reading and writing skills.

The ability to find, select, and process information has never been more important. Knowledge is no longer static and in many ways most facts that are 'learnt' will become increasingly rapidly redundant. Adults in this century must continuously modify their existing knowledge and find new information if they are to be able to cope with what has been called the 'information explosion'. (In Britain alone 35 000 *new* books are published each year and since Newton's time the amount of information has increased by a *factor* of one million!) The institutionalized, traditional transmission of knowledge ceases for most people at sixteen when they leave school and for some at twenty-two when they leave college. After that people have to learn on their own. People who have not got the necessary skills may become frustrated and will not be truly capable of taking part in the development of society. As educationalists we must teach our pupils skills so that they can learn for themselves.

Finding out information from libraries, books, and periodicals is as much an activity of a working scientist as is practical work. Scientists, in general, spend 4–5 hours a week reading, and, on average, read about ten different periodicals (2, pp. 65–6). The library is a key part of any research estabishment. If we wish our pupils to experience what it is like to be a working scientist then finding information in books and journals must be part of that experience. For those pupils who go on to Higher Education, the confident use of a library, catalogue, indexes, etc. will be absolutely essential.

Pupils who are involved in any resource-based learning will need these skills; setting pupils tasks to find out information without such skill training will be very frustrating for the pupil and put an intolerable burden on the teacher and librarian in providing simultaneous 'help' for a whole class of pupils. (Teachers sometimes try to have science lessons in a library, assuming their pupils have library skills, and can be very disconcerted at the chaos that ensues.)

Using libraries and books to find information can be fun: it is like a game and pupils can get a lot of satisfaction finding out in this way. In some respects it is more secure than doing an experiment where there is an element of doubt about the validity of the information found. It is good that pupils should feel that there are different ways of finding information, sometimes an experiment is the only source and sometimes only a book will have the answer. Alison Kelly makes a point of girls' ability to work with the written word. As this is a scientifically valid way of working, girls may perhaps enjoy science more as a result.

'Girls, on average, have greater verbal skills than boys, and they frequently perform better in written work.' (3, p. 278)

In a major survey conducted by the British Library Research and Development team many teachers were asked about their ideas on the library-user skills necessary for the effective learning of their subject by pupils. The interviewers found that very frequently teachers said, 'I suppose we ought to be teaching this' (4, p. 15). This study looked at the library-user education programmes that already exist in schools. They found that about half the schools had one or more lesson in the first year devoted to learning library skills (half therefore had NO lessons!) and some had one lesson a week. This lesson was often called the 'library lesson' and was usually isolated from subjects such as science, and was rarely reinforced in any subject other than English.

Those schools that did have a programme in the first year usually included this content:

Content	*Methods*
Layout of library	pointing; guided tour; pupils
Borrowing procedures, opening hours, rules	drawing their own plan, talk; demonstration; handout
Subject index	talk; chart; worksheet; handout
Catalogue of library stock	talk; handout; worksheet
Classification scheme	talk; chart; handout .
Search terms	question and answer session; demonstration with books
Alphabetical/numerical order	talk; blackboard demonstration; worksheet; practical exercise; reshelving books
Shelf arrangements (fiction, non-fiction, pamphlets, oversize books, periodicals, audio-visual materials)	pointing; handout; reshelving; worksheet; quiz; practical; demonstration
Finding items on shelves	talk; handout; worksheet; quiz; treasure hut
Parts of a book	talk; handout; worksheet, blackboard
Using books (contents, index, notes)	talk; handout; worksheet
Reference books	talk; handout; worksheet; exercises with cards
Bibliographies	worksheet; practical exercises
Project planning and implementation	talk; handout; execution of library project

There was a marked absence of audio-visual aids in the teaching for most programmes.   (4, p. 8)

'After their first year, pupils received little formal library-user education. If it could be shown that the introductory courses run by librarians were reinforced in subsequent years, with additions made widely during subject teaching, there would be no cause for concern. Interviews with teachers confirmed that this was not being done to any great degree, however, although needs for subsequent instruction were expressed by most teachers interviewed.'   (4, p. 13)

The second year sometimes provided revision and some additional skills, the third year had very little instruction. In the fourth and fifth year:

'When time was available, pupils embarking on examination courses were taken through the stages of producing projects. This was done superficially, usually in one school period, and with very few exceptions, the librarian was not directly involved in the supervision of projects.' (4, p. 13)

HMI also commented on the lack of use of libraries by fourth and especially fifth formers (5). In the sixth form although teachers realized that much greater demands were being made on sixth formers' study skills only 'brief and basic introductions to advanced library materials were given'.

It is clear from this study that not enough is being done for pupils and what is being done in the library is not being reinforced by subjects such as science.

The library is one of the most expensive resources in a school, especially if it has a fully qualified librarian. It provides many valuable facilities that are often unknown and under-used.

Facilities that can be provided by the library
1 The expertise of the librarian.
2 Purchase of books for library and help for science department.
3 Borrowing of books from other libraries.
4 Access to the British Library.
5 Preparation of learning materials.
6 Periodicals.
7 Teacher education.
8 Catalogue (of all resources in the school?)
9 System for pupils to borrow books.
10 Source of audio-visual aids.

As scientists we should use the benefits of these facilities to help the learning of science by our pupils. Their science and general education will be helped by the reinforcing of information skills.

Problems

1 *Library skills*

A major problem that has to be faced when there is any new addition to the curriculum of a department is whether there is enough time to teach it. Fortunately the amount of time teaching study skills need take from science lessons is slight. Indeed it might ultimately save time that is normally spent 'going over' work, or in rather ineffective teacher-help to individuals who with skills-training could work on their own. For most schools, using library skills in science lessons will be only a reinforcement of what the pupils have learnt already and would require only one or two lessons in the library. Homeworks and other assignments, especially for the faster pupil, can be set that require further use of these skills. However, although time might easily be found in a science course, access to the library can be a problem. Class lessons have to be booked in advance and a trail of bright pupils to the library to do research on topics can cause difficulties if the library is shut or the librarian too busy. Often there is restricted access for pupils at break and lunch which might make problems for library-based homeworks. The physical location of the library can make things difficult if pupils have to walk from one end of a building to another.

Before pupils can gain any value from books they must, of course, be able to read them! Information skills are totally bound up with advanced reading skills such as skimming and scanning (p. 19). It is a sad feature of many of the library-user programmes that:

'Teachers are more concerned with book usage than book retrieval yet book retrieval was the main content of the library-user courses.' (4, p. 17)

Without adequate reading skills any information skills development is bound to fail.

It is very difficult to have a good selection of books on science in the library. Often there are quite a range of good books for the more able pupil and then a selection of predominantly picture books for the others. It is hard to find books on scientific topics that have a good text—often the pictures are so enticing that pupils do not actually read but only look. More popular books and interesting articles from papers might be more stimulating.

Although most pupils only receive an introduction to information skills which as scientists we need to develop and reinforce, two groups of pupils seem particularly under-educated: those pupils who do projects (see later sections) and sixth formers. Sixth formers have much more independent study and a much more complex task than pupils lower down the school. They use many more reference books and can no longer expect to find all the answers to their questions in one or two textbooks. Long essays and some long projects are frequently given as assignments requiring many hours of data collection before the essay can be written. Free periods mean that work must be done in the hurly burly of school and finding a quiet place to work can be difficult. Despite the great differences in learning styles most sixth formers get no instruction in how to cope with the different strategies they now need. For many it is a case of trial and error and of facing a disappointed or disapproving teacher after each essay has been marked. Teachers often try to help their pupils individually *after* the essay has been completed but this is very demoralising and unsatisfactory. It is quite unusual for sixth form pupils to use any periodicals for their assignments—even though this will be a vital part of their work at college.

Identifying and articulating what information is needed is a skill that many pupils do not have. Often pupils may be so ignorant of the nature of the assignment they have been set that it is difficult for them to know where to start and how to ask the librarian for help. This quote from an article written by two school librarians seems only too familiar.

'We meet many fourth and fifth-year pupils embarking on projects for their 16 + and CSE examinations without any clear idea of their purpose, except that the project is a necessary component of their final examinations. Yet all have been briefed by their subject teachers on organising a logical sequence of work into chapters, including an introduction and conclusion, and so on. Faced with the library shelves and a choice of information sources, many just do not know where to begin. How many times each week do we have conversations rather like this one with pupils in our libraries?

'What are you looking for, John?'
'Dunno really, just something to start my project off.'
'What's your project going to be about?'
'It's about railways.'
'What sort of things do you need to know about railways?'
'Dunno, sir.'   (6, p. 215)

Sometimes the information is just not there. I had one group of first years who were interested in the reproductive behaviour of mammals who lived in water. Despite quite vigorous and thoughtful research in encyclopaedias and other specialized books in the library the answers to their questions were not to be found. Teachers, quite frequently, set assignments where the information is extremely difficult to find and this can cause a lot of frustration in their pupils. The problem of how much success we should give our pupils is a very important one for their education; instant and universal success, however motivating, is not a very good preparation for life and yet constant frustration can only lead to disillusionment and a sense of failure. As teachers we must know when we give assignments or respond to the pupils' ideas for assignments whether they will have easy success, success after perseverance, or no success at all. Pupils must learn how to cope with difficulty and with failure, but the teacher must plan for difficulty as well as success and be able to turn failure from frustration into an aspect of education.

2 Book-user skills

Finding information from a book requires reading skills. The British Library research team found that pupils did not have the necessary skills:

'The internal structure of a book did not appear to be explained by many librarians. Those who did covered the parts of a book: title page, contents list, chapters and index, mentioning briefly how to use the index in order to find specific information in the text. However, many children apparently fail to use the appropriate reading strategies which are essential for the effective use of books. Librarians are not reading teachers and did not therefore link reading strategies to using books in the library. It should be stated here that most teachers are not reading teachers either, so that few first-year pupils are well equipped to make full use of library materials. A pupil may listen to comments about a book's index, and how it notes the relevant pages to check; but he will have great difficulty in extracting information from the book unless he appreciates that it is proper behaviour to skim and scan these relevant pages, and is given confidence through encouragement in using such strategies. (4, p. 5)

Teachers must know the books the pupils are to use; simple dictionaries suitable for younger pupils do not always have the scientific words we have asked the pupils to find. It is also very sad and confusing to find that pupils have laboriously copied definitions from dictionaries that are totally inappropriate: 'elements' for example—the four elements, earth, fire, water, air; 'atmosphere'; 'solutions' all with the non-scientific meaning, or with definitions that are far too hard to be understood for example:

'*Catalyst*
Any substance whose presence alters the rate of a chemical reaction whilst remaining unchanged in its own chemical composition at the end of the reaction is a catalyst. The term is normally used in conjunction with those substances that increase reaction rates (positive catalysts), although it is also applicable to those that slow down the reaction rate (negative catalysts or inhibitors). (7)

(This quote comes from a book specially written for non-chemists.)

3 Projects

'We award the highest academic accolade to a student who can see a question, focus it into an enquiry, trace sources, find relevant information in those sources, collate the information, reorganize that information in a way that meets the question posed, and write up the reorganized material as a report. To those who achieve that pinnacle of scholarship we award a Ph.D. This same process is the one we have adopted as the main teaching method for the less academic and less well motivated school pupil, almost completely in the humanities, and extensively even in the crafts and sciences. Yet we often give no specific help. The 'project method' is felt to motivate inherently, and this motivation is supposed to solve all learning problems. No wonder projects are often so feeble.'   (8, p. 208)

Projects are a common method of assessment in science CSE examinations and there are some advocates of project work as a method of scientific teaching. There are, however, major drawbacks in using projects as the main vehicle of science education. If projects are open-ended and largely unstructured it is difficult to ensure that teaching objectives are being fulfilled and basic skills are being taught. It is also a very demanding form of teaching unless pupils are well-versed in information, reading, and writing skills. Teachers can be totally overwhelmed by constant cries for attention or very disappointed in the 'feeble' product of weeks of work. Professor Eggleston is even more scathing than Michael Marland in his condemnation of projects.

'It is possible for a child to go through a continuing succession of projects; in each one reaching minimal achievement; attaining no more than an incomplete and hazy understanding, and often a very great deal of frustration. The project method offers no kind of mechanism whereby mastery, incremental learning or even certainty of progress can be ensured.'   (9)

Sadly, sometimes in our teaching we ask our pupils to move from one extreme demand to another—and this is especially so for the less able. In the lower school many pupils have a diet of worksheets where the questions have already been asked and they, in effect, fill in the missing words. Then suddenly in the fourth and fifth year, they are required to do a completely unstructured project requiring at an advanced level all the skills that the worksheet has been designed to avoid developing! It is little wonder that many fail.

It is difficult for teachers to have a schedule for training pupils in project and essay-writing work. Very often we might say to pupils, 'Write an essay about water for homework' without thinking of the difficult skills such a task requires.

Projects can be a valuable teaching strategy providing pupils have developed the skills needed to cope with such a vast task and providing the teacher has a programme so that projects develop from the simple, needing only a few skills already mastered, to the more open-ended. Indeed it is only by doing projects that the full range of information skills can be used and tried. The ability to do projects is the hallmark of the successful independent learner.

Strategies

1 *Libraries*

The science department cannot work alone in developing information skills and without a whole-school policy pupils will not be taught or practise these skills sufficiently for them to become independent learners. The British Library research team have produced an 'ideal' library-user education programme (4, see Appendix C). In this model, all the attitudes, knowledge, and skills would be introduced during the first year. During subsequent years, these would be continually reinforced and treated in a depth more appropriate to the developing learner. A piece of research (i.e. a project) requires the same *range* of skills and abilities irrespective of pupils' age. The difference lies in the *level* to which the skills are developed. In practice, it means that the whole range of skills should be introduced—some taught specifically and some diffused across the curriculum in a range of different contexts. This can only be achieved if a plan is drafted, objectives defined, and areas of responsibility marked out by an overall co-ordinator, librarian or teacher. In theory (and practice) the balance falls in favour of the chartered librarian, the person *most* in touch with the library materials.

The *timing* for adoption of any or all of the elements in the model would be decided by the teacher—elements (or modules) could be introduced into subject teaching as and when required. The science department can make a most valuable contribution to this programme by setting its own library assignments.

The following are examples of worksheets that are directly related to library usage.

HOW TO FIND OUT CHART

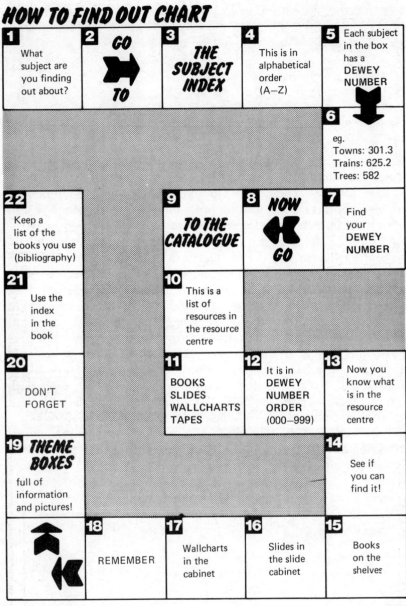

| 1 What subject are you finding out about? | 2 GO TO | 3 THE SUBJECT INDEX | 4 This is in alphabetical order (A–Z) | 5 Each subject in the box has a DEWEY NUMBER |

| 6 eg. Towns: 301.3 Trains: 625.2 Trees: 582 |

| 22 Keep a list of the books you use (bibliography) | 9 TO THE CATALOGUE | 8 NOW GO | 7 Find your DEWEY NUMBER |

| 21 Use the index in the book | 10 This is a list of resources in the resource centre |

| 20 DON'T FORGET | 11 BOOKS SLIDES WALLCHARTS TAPES | 12 It is in DEWEY NUMBER ORDER (000–999) | 13 Now you know what is in the resource centre |

| 19 THEME BOXES full of information and pictures! | 14 See if you can find it! |

| 18 REMEMBER | 17 Wallcharts in the cabinet | 16 Slides in the slide cabinet | 15 Books on the shelves |

(10)

LIBRARY

QUIZ QUIZ QUIZ

START HERE

1. All fiction books in the library are arranged in *Alphabetical* order of their author's surname.

   Put the following names into *Alphabetical* order.

   Richards
   Chambers
   Smith
   Dawson
   Benson
   Thompson

2. Look up Rosemary Sutcliffe in the *Author* catalogue.

   How many books are listed by her?
   Name two of them

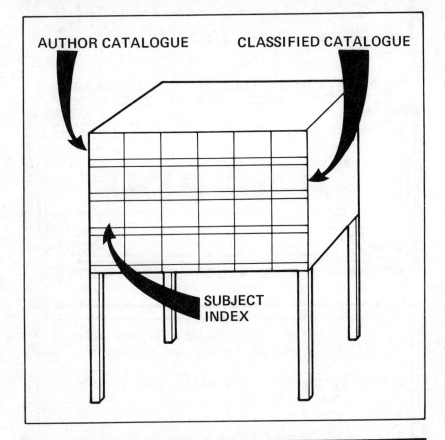

AUTHOR CATALOGUE   CLASSIFIED CATALOGUE

SUBJECT INDEX

3. All the non fiction books are arranged on the shelves in subject groups.
   Each subject has a number.
   This is called the *Dewey* system.

4. To find the *Dewey* number for a subject you need to look in the *Subject index*

SUBJECT INDEX

5. Find the *Dewey* number for

Birds
Rugby
Motor cycles
Costume

in the *Subject Index*

6. Using the *Classified* catalogue choose one of the subjects above and find the places for it in the *Classified* catalogue. How many books are there listed on your subject?

7. Need to relax? Choose a film loop, sit back and look at it on the film loop projector.

Moving from the catalogues to the shelves~

8. Answer the questions on **one** of the following books.

Weather and Life by Alan Hammersley. 551.59

(a) What is the title to Chapter 5?
(b) What page does Chapter 5 begin on?
(c) What causes a sunset? (Use the index at the end of the book.)

or

Search and rescue by Nancy Martin. 614.8

(a) What is the title to Chapter 6?
(b) What page does Chapter 6 begin on?
(c) What were owlers? (Use the index at the end of the book.)

REFERENCE BOOKS

Reference Books are the ones you can't borrow.

All the *Reference Books* have a mark on the spine. What is it?

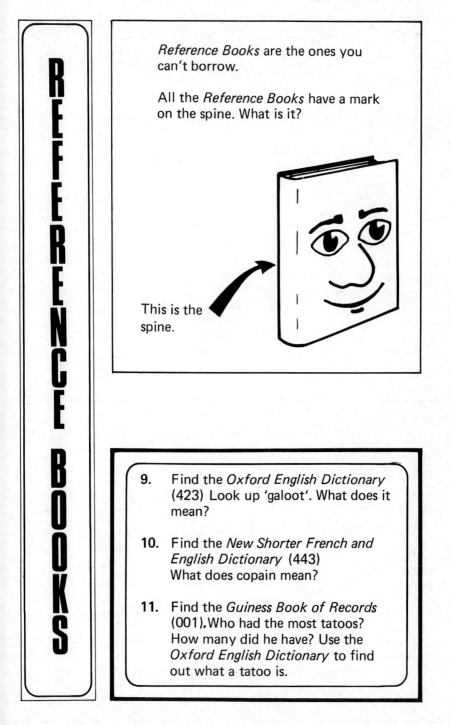

This is the spine.

9. Find the *Oxford English Dictionary* (423) Look up 'galoot'. What does it mean?

10. Find the *New Shorter French and English Dictionary* (443) What does copain mean?

11. Find the *Guiness Book of Records* (001). Who had the most tatoos? How many did he have? Use the *Oxford English Dictionary* to find out what a tatoo is.

FINDING THINGS IN ENCYCLOPEDIAS

In the last volume of each encyclopedia there is a long index which tells you all the places in the encyclopedia where you can find the information you need

When you look up a subject you will find something like this—

> **DOG** domesticated animal found in nearly every part of the world inhabited by man. 6.103. hound 9.115. performing dogs 13. 139.

This means that the main article on dogs is in volume 6 page 103. For the other aspects of the subject you will need to look in the other volumes mentioned.

The index in *Children's Britannica* is in volume 20. In the *Oxford Junior Encyclopedia* it is in volume 13.

Use these two encyclopedias to answer the following questions..................

12. Look up Hopscotch in both encylopedias. Draw the pattern given in *Children's Britannica.* Draw another pattern given in the *Oxford Junior Encyclopedia.*

13. Look up 'husk' in the index of both encyclopedias. In which volumes can you find out things about huskies?

14. Look up the Pied Piper of Hamelin and briefly describe his story. Do either of the encyclopedias tell you from which country the story comes?

REMEMBER THAT THE LIBRARY IS ALSO A

This means that it contains slides, film loops, charts, newspaper cuttings and records as well as books.

15. Which newspapers does the library take?

16. Name three magazines which the library takes.

17. What is a Jackdaw? Choose one and write down its title. What does it contain?

18. What is the Local History file? What sort of material does it contain?

19. Where are the information trays and boxes kept? Name one of them and list what is in it.

20. Find the map chest and look at some of the charts in it. Is it arranged in the same way as the rest of the library?

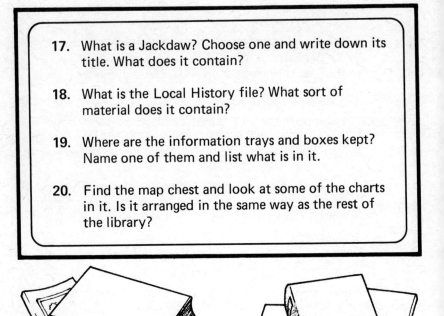

When you have completed this quiz you should have a good idea of the types of information which you can find in the library to help with your work.

Put this booklet into your folder, you may need to use it again.

SCIENCE!
LIBRARY

MAMMALS THAT LIVE IN HOT DESERTS:

1. Name *three mammals* that live in the *hot desert*

2. What are *rodents?*

3. How do these animals keep cool?

4. Where do they get their water?

5. What do they eat?

6. Why can camels survive in the desert?

EITHER

     use dictionaries and encyclopedias in the
     reference section
     dictionaries at 423
     general encyclopedias at 030
     science encyclopedias at 500
     animals encyclopedias at 590–599
OR   loans section at 590–599

Finding the Book You Want: An Algorithm

Sylvia Stagg and Sarah Brew, Librarians, Sevenoaks School , Kent

IT WAS THE advent of our new school library which stimulated us into re-thinking the way in which we introduced boys to the use of the library catalogue. We thought it would be a good opportunity to reinforce the initial talks on using the catalogue which are given to all boys when they first come to the school. In addition we had new catalogue furniture and a newly compiled visible subject index which the boys had not seen, so we were looking for a simple method of drawing attention to these and at the same time providing a permanent guide to this valuable key to the stock of the library. We thought of many ways of doing this and eventually settled on an algorithm as being the most effective solution.

An algorithm is a way of presenting complicated instructions or procedures.It does so by means of a flow-chart so designed that it forsees every contingency that can be encountered by anyone following it. One of the reasons for choosing this way was that it was acceptable to boys of all ages. Sixth-formers respected it and eleven-year-old first-formers enjoyed using it as a plan of action when set book-finding games. In the form of a large chart it is on view alongside the catalogue and it is also available as a duplicated handout.

The algorithm shown is designed specifically as a guide to this school's catalogue and subject index, but it could easily be adapted for any other. It deals only with our books but a similar guide could and will be devised for our audio-visual aids.

Although the final result should appear very simple and straightforward, we should warn that algorithms are time-consuming to prepare, and the principles involved need to be clearly understood. We were fortunate in that Sarah Brew's husband is a computer expert and he vetted our flow-charting techniques.The boys themselves finally tested and approved our algorithm.

Reference
WHEATLEY, D.M. and UNWIN, W.W. *The algorithm writer's guide.* Longman, 1972, ISBN 582 42162 4.

Source: Stagg, S. and Brew, S. (1977). "Finding the book you want: an algorithm." *School Librarian,* Vol.25,pt.3,pp221-222.

(10)

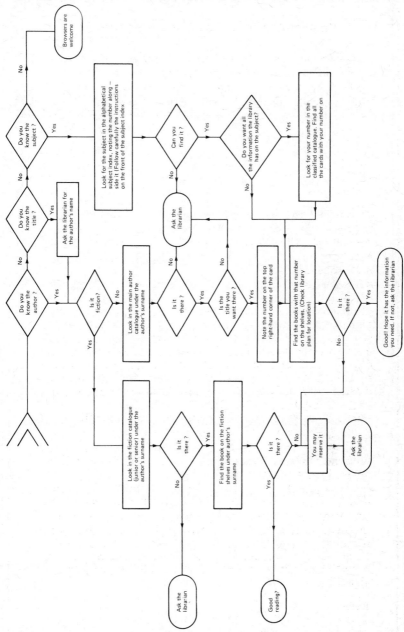

(10)

Use your dictionary

Words in a dictionary are arranged in ALPHABETICAL ORDER.
1　Write down these words in your book in alphabetical order
　　(a)　neuter, newton, neutron, neutrino, neutral, neuron.
　　(b)　molecular, molar, molecule, modal, mode, molecular weight, molecular mass, mole, mollusc.

The Rock Salt Experiment

New words

Using a dictionary find out what these words mean and write down their meanings in YOUR OWN WORDS.
1　Solution
2　Solvent
3　Dissolve
4　Evaporate
5　Crystals
6　Soluble
7　Filter
8　Insoluble
9　Apparatus
10　Pure

Other simple assignments can be set once the retrieval skills are learnt, for example:

1　When did Sir Isaac Newton live?
2　What was the title of the most famous book written by Darwin?
3　What is a carnivore? Make a list of six carnivores.

etc.

Ideally, with the discussions over the last five years on language across the curriculum, many schools will already have a whole-school language policy, but if this has not got off the ground, liaison with the English department and the library is extremely important. Each should know what the other is doing with the pupils so that science can build on the framework laid down by English teachers and the librarian. The librarian should have a copy of the science syllabus and schemes of work so that she knows what the pupils have covered and what are the resources needed in the future. Class lessons in the library will probably have to be booked in advance, but also she should be warned well in advance of assignments that will be set that will need information from the library. (It is not easy to provide 300 pupils with information on dinosaurs for their week's homework!) Any arrangement that is made between the science department and more-able pupils so that they can use the library as a resource should be carefully planned and given the librarian's consent. Similar skills can be practised by the librarian providing a box of books on loan to the science department and therefore save a lot of pupil movement. Projects in the fourth and fifth year should be planned by pupil, teacher, *and* librarian if it involves a lot of library-based information.

Libraries are as useful as their selection of books. Science teachers often neglect this aspect of school provision—or keep all the good books within the department. Within my science department I keep only selections of textbooks and all books of any general interest are housed in the school library. Collections of books that are relevant to the work of the moment are withdrawn from the school library. Libraries need more books with interesting texts on subjects that will interest the pupil without the overuse of pictures to gain their attention. Many school libraries have few books on the effects of science for readers at any level. (Information on books can be found at the Book Information Service which is part of the National Book League. In each major public library there is someone who is responsible for childen's books. The central LEA librarian or library can also be a very useful source of ideas and titles.) Health and hobby magazines with quite a high science content are becoming more common and more popular. Titles such as *Gardening World*, *Electronics Today*, *Computing Today*, and *Here's Health* to name a few could be stocked. (An appeal to the PTA might reveal some pupils and parents who subscribe who would be happy to donate back copies to the library.)

There should be a common catalogue between the library and other school departments including science so that the resources of the school are accessible to all and pupils need cope with only one cataloguing system. This should also include non-book material. It saves a lot of teacher time and lost books if pupils borrow science books from the library (not, of course, textbooks) where there is a ready-made lending system. Copies of all the science textbooks issued should be kept in the reference section of the library for pupil use in school.

2　*Using books*

Once again it must be said that using books to find information depends entirely on the pupil's ability to formulate the right questions (if that has not already been done in the assignment), to use skills such as skimming and scanning to locate the information on the page, and to use reflective reading techniques to locate and understand the information itself. Many information sources can be rejected very early on in a search thus narrowing down the vast field available and making it much easier for the pupil to focus their attention onto potentially useful sources.

Many aspects of a book provide information on its contents before any real reading has been attempted. Title, author, publisher, date of publication, 'blurb', cover design, contents page, index, glossary, and preface all provide very valuable clues that the pupil should be able to recognize.

Exercises on looking at covers, contents pages, book blurbs, etc. can be set. Collections of books that illustrate good and bad features and different levels of information can be shown to the pupils so that pupils can learn to quickly assess books from the publishing details and covers alone. This assessment skill will save them an immense amount of time when faced with a well-stocked library. Most pupils can use an index and this can be practised. Here are some examples of worksheets that help develop book-user skills.

Taking in Information

Reading

When you are given an assignment to complete which requires you to locate books which have not necessarily been recommended to you, the appearance and sheer weight of some of the books you may choose from the relevant shelves in the library may confuse and deter you. However, after the initial shock, try to remember that **most** books are written to some sort of plan. For example, the main idea of the book can perhaps be broken down into the individual chapter themes. These in turn, may break down into main ideas for sections, which themselves, may possibly be divided into specific ideas for each paragraph.

So, given that some sort of plan exists within the book, how do you find out enough about the book to tell whether it may be of value to you? Well, quick information about a book is provided by:—

Title
■ perhaps gives the general subject area;
■ perhaps gives the level of approach (although sometimes indicated more by a subtitle).

Author's name
■ you may recognize him as an authority;
■ you may know what he has written before;
■ his qualifications may be listed.

Book cover
■ may provide a summary or review of the book;

■ may provide critics' comments;
■ may provide information on the author's qualifications, experience etc.

Publishing date
■ be aware of the difference between the edition date, and the date when the book was first published;
■ may suggest a clue to the current reliability of the book.

Preface (Foreword, Author's remarks, Introduction)
■ may suggest for whom the book is written;
■ may suggest the scope and purpose of the book;
■ may discuss the outline and structure used;
■ may suggest how to use the book.

Table of contents
■ may detail the general coverage of the book;
■ may provide a clue to the organisation and relationship of the topics and sub-topics.

Index
■ provides specific references, thus saving time reading the whole book;
■ may provide links to alternative terms e.g. *'see also . . .'*

Chapter headings
■ these organise the book's main ideas into sections.

Summary (either chapter or whole book summaries)
■ usually draws together the main threads of what has been written. May be in point form, and concisely worded.

Keep in the fore of your mind the purpose of your study i.e. why you need the book—and so concern yourself with discovering whether the whole book or a section of the book may meet your needs.

So, having obtained an overall perspective of the book, and having decided on, say, a section which might be useful, then **survey** that section, looking at such aspects as:—

- **Boldface type (or italics)** e.g. emphasising 'key' words or sentences;
- **Pictures with captions.** These may help to explain the material you need;
- **Charts.** These may provide a great deal of information at a glance;
- **Maps and diagrams.** These may provide 'potted' information, thus condensing several pages of writing into one 'picture';
- **First and last paragraphs.** These may indicate what is, or just has been, discussed;
- **Headings and subheadings.** These may give further clues to the structure of ideas.

At this point, you should start raising **questions** which will enable you to have a specific purpose for reading this section. For example, subheadings in the section may themselves provide the basis for questions to be answered. Or, you may simply decide to locate the author's main ideas and argument. You are really setting yourself a target to be attained by reading the section—i.e. *'what am I particularly going to look for when I am reading these pages?'* Having then decided that this section is worthwhile reading, and having formulated some sort of target to be achieved in your reading, then you can proceed to **read** and **take notes.**

Reproduced from 'Studying—a practical guide for students of all ages', published by the National Youth Bureau, 17–23 Albion Street, Leicester LE1 6GD (ISBN 0 902095 39 0).   (10)

Which Books Do I Need?
Titles and Covers

Titles

Introduction to Materials Science, by B. R. Schlenker, John Wiley, 1974.

Materials Science (2nd Edition) by J. C. Anderson, K. D. Leaver, J. M. Alexander and R. D. Rawlings, Nelson, 1974.

Materials in Industry, by W. J. Patton, Prentice-Hall, 1968.

Structure and Metals, by Michael Hudson, Hutchinson Educational, 1973.

Fibre-Reinforced Materials Technology, by N. J. Parratt, Van Nostrand, 1972.

The Structure and Properties of Materials, Vol. 3, 'Mechanical Behavior', by H. W. Hayden, W. G. Moffatt and J. Wulff. John Wiley, 1965.

Strength of Materials, by Peter Black. Pergamon Press, 1966.

History of the Strength of Materials, by S. P. Timoshenko. McGraw-Hill, 1953.

Strong Solids, by A. Kelly. Oxford University Press, 1966.

The Mechanical Properties of Matter, by A. H. Cottrell. John Wiley, current edition.

Formulas for Stress and Strain, by R. J. Roark. MCGraw-Hill, current edition. (This is the bible of do-it-yourself stressing.)

Less technical books

Philosophy of Structures, by E. Torroja (translated from the Spanish). University of California Press, Berkeley, 1962.

Metals in the Service of Man, by W. Alexander and A. Street. Penguin Books—current edition.

On Growth and Form, by D'Arcy Thompson (abridged edition). Cambridge University Press, 1961. (This is the classic account of the shape and structure of animals, originally published in 1917 but still readable and important.)

Biomechanics, by R. McNeil Alexander. Chapman and Hall, 1975.

Mechanical Design of Organisms, by S. A. Wainwright, W. D. Biggs, J. D. Currey and J. M. Gosline, Edward Arnold, 1976.

The Southseaman, by J. Weston Matyr. Blackwood, 1928. (An excellent account of classical wooden shipbuilding in the 1920s.)

Engineering Metals and their Alloys, by C. H. Samans, Macmillan, New York, 1953. (This is a good general account of practical metallurgy, rather more advanced than *Metals in the Service of Man*, but very comprehensible and readable.)

Ceramic and Graphite Fibers and Whiskers, by McCreight, Rauch and Sutton. Academic Press, New York, 1965.

Structures or Why Things Don't Fall Down, by J. E. Gordon. Penguin Books, 1978.

Finally, *The History of Technology* (Oxford University Press, 1954) is a mine of information on all matters connected with the history of materials and structures. This is a forty-guinea five-volume book which is available in many public libraries.

Look at these titles.

Answer these questions.

1 Which book would you choose to find out about the uses of metals?
2 Which book/s would you choose to give you the most up-to-date information on structure in plants?
3 Which book would answer the question 'why have cows got four legs?'
4 Which book might answer the question 'what keeps up a suspension bridge?'
5 Which book might you choose if you were trying to build a concrete bridge?

Answer these questions.

Look at the collection of books. Only look at their *covers*.

6 Which book would give you most general information about metals?
7 Which book would be the most amusing to read? Would it also be useful for answering questions on metals?
8 Which book is the oldest? Is it likely to be too out-of-date for a project on plastics?
9 Which book would be most useful if you were making something?
10 Which book would be most useful to a specialist in the history of working with metals?

(10)

ANIMAL CLASSIFICATION—FISH
1. Look up FISH in the subject index.
2. What is the Dewey Classification number?
3. Find the shelf in the library where there are books on fish.
4. Write down the name of a book that would tell you about sharks.
5. Look at the contents page of this book. Will this book tell you about
   (a) the different types of shark?
   (b) the life story of sharks?
   (c) where killer sharks can be found in the world?
   (d) the size of killer sharks?
   (e) how many people have been killed by sharks in the sea around Australia?
   (f) the teeth of the shark?
6. Choose one of these topics that is in this book and write down two facts about sharks that interested you—IN YOUR OWN WORDS.

Which book do I need?

Contents pages

Look at the contents pages of these three biology books:

Projects in Biology
Contents

Introduction	xi	
1 Can human inheritance be predicted?	1	
Sampling the population for the ability to tongue-roll or taste a chemical substance.		
How does hair vary?	4	
An investigation into the differences in hair structure.		
3 What effects hair setting?		

Testing the natural elasticity of hair and its ability to set temporarily and 'permanently'. 7
4 What clothing keeps us warmest? 11
A tin can is used as a model of the human body so that the loss of heat through clothing materials of different colours, textures and thicknesses can be measured.

It's your life
Contents

Answer these questions.
1. Which book is the most 'high powered'? Why do you think this?
2. Which book would you choose if you were studying O level Biology? Explain why?
3. Which book will have the most experiments in it?
4. Which book will tell you most about
   (a) birth control
   (b) germs
   (c) hygiene
   (d) teeth
   (e) breathing in mammals.
5. Which book would you choose because it seems the most interesting? Explain your choice.

Using an index

Weedkillers 337
Weighing 24
  by difference 24
Wine 282

Xenon 35
X-rays 65–7

Zinc 222, 238
  carbonate 236

chloride 236
hydroxide 236
manufacture 230
occurrence 222
oxide 235
physical properties 231
reactions 232
sulphate 233, 236
uses 233

Look at this index and answer these questions.
1 What page/s would you look at to find out about—
  (a) sulphur
  (b) a valency table
  (c) the hardness of water
  (d) what zinc is used for
  (e) how sulphuric(VI) acid is made
  (f) the difference between thermal dissociations and decomposition
  (g) sulphates.

(14)

Which Book Do I Need?

Do some research in your groups on how books are organised. Choose three or four non-fiction books from your library and fill in a report about each. Your report could be arranged like this:

Title:
  is the title a helpful guide to the content of the book?
Author
Publisher
Date of publication
Any reprints
Cover:
  is there a blurb?
  is it helpful?
Contents list:
  is there one?
  are the headings very general?
  do the headings really tell you what each chapter or section
    is about?

Index:
　is there one?
　how is it arranged?
　does it give cross-references?
　how?
　is it easy to use?
　is it detailed enough?
　does it list illustrations?
List of illustrations:
　is there one?
　is it helpful?
　are the illustrations placed just anywhere in the text?
　are they close to the passage which goes with them?
Glossary:
　is there one?
　is one needed?
　how is it arranged?
　alphabetically?
　by numbers?
　are there notes at the bottom of the page?
　at the end of each section?
Bibliography:
　is there one?
　are all the relevant details of books given?
　are there any further notes about books which might be
　　helpful?

If you find that a book is very poorly organized, then you should write to the publisher and suggest improvements. Details of how to do that are given in Unit 12 'Writing a letter'.

(15)

Once the book has been selected and the relevant section has been identified there still remains the problem of how to tackle long sections of a book. One method that works well is to ask pupils to follow this sequence:

1 Look at the chapter heading, each page quickly, any pictures or diagrams.
2 Read the introduction and summary if they are there, otherwise the first and last pages of the chapter.
3 Skim chapter quickly.
4 Read the introduction and summary (etc.) again.

5 Read the chapter more carefully, locating the main idea of the paragraphs, and taking notes if required.
6 Read the beginning and end of the chapter again.

Pupils need practice at selecting information. Initially this will have been done by the teacher but in later assignments the pupil should select and be able to justify his or her selection.

3 Assignments

Setting good assignments, ranging from simple homeworks to large-scale projects, is of immense importance to our pupils. In a very profound book on the School Library, an American, Ann Davis writes

The assignment is the '*key to teaching and learning* ... (*and*) *largely determines what pupils do and how they do it; hence it determines the results achieved.*'
The quality of the assignment directly influences the success or failure of the learning endeavor. 'Evidence ... shows that vague, indefinite assignments that lack the power to motivate are common causes of children's failure to learn.' (16, p. 206*)

She goes on to say ominously but accurately, 'Poor assignments are evidence of a serious teacher disability'.

Before setting assignments she proposes that teachers ask themselves the following questions that will help the teacher set better assignments. (This is reprinted in full in Appendix B, p. 78.)

Is this assignment educationally significant and worthy of the student's attention?
Will it create and sustain an interest in learning?
Does it grow out of the course objectives?
Is it essential and at the right time in the course?
Is it at the right level?
Does it take a reasonable amount of time and effort?
Will pupils of different abilities be able to cope?
Are there appropriate resources readily available and in sufficient quantity?
Is it clear enough so that it can be understood?

'Is the assignment dependent on the utilization of new learning skills, new reference tools and techniques?
The teacher has the obligation to foresee the skills necessary for the completion of an assigned task. A competent teacher plans to equip the students to work intelligently and efficiently by introducing or having the librarian introduce the skills and techniques essential to building the skill level of performance demanded by each assignment.' (16, p. 208)*

*Reprinted with permission of the R.R. Bowker Company from *The School Library: A force for educational excellence* by Ruth A. Davies. © 1969 by Xerox Corporation.

Before pupils begin doing project work they must be able to use the requisite skills competently. This means that early in their science course they should have a programme of reading exercises (such as DARTS, p. 39) that will develop their skimming, scanning, and reflective reading. Pupils should be able to select from prose the information they require. Library and book-user skills will help them to find and evaluate likely sources of information. Note-making should be part of the skills they use in science all the time to record information. All these skills are vital for attempting any project.

It is always a good idea to show to the pupils good and bad examples of any new type of work. Good and bad projects and project plans can be discussed by small groups of the pupils. Before pupils begin major projects (not just small homework assignments) where they will be expected to work for quite a few hours, often on their own, the teacher should discuss with the pupils the length, how long it should take to produce, the level of detail that might be reached, and the potential audience. With longer projects the teacher must monitor the progress of the pupils otherwise there is much loss of time and often a poor product. (Do not allow pupils to work secretly—who say everything is 'fine' and 'at home'!)

Projects vary from the easy to the very difficult indeed and clearly there must be a gradation from easy to hard. (Teachers do not always appreciate this, however, and do set first year pupils essays on *'water'* etc. It is only the pupils inability to do such an essay that limits such an overpowering subject.) Below is a series of factors that determine the ease of a project. Whether the project is easy or not is almost entirely determined by how the teacher and pupil see the project. Following this list of factors there are three examples of projects: easy, moderate, and hard.

1 *Closed topics* are much easier than open-ended projects. There is very much less selection and evaluation; information merely has to be found and written down. Finding facts, dates, numerical data and copying diagrams are all simple closed tasks.

2 *Shorter topics* where there is only a very limited amount of information to be found are much more suitable for younger pupils who will only have a very limited amount of time. Homework is not usually more than an hour a week in science and teachers have to bear in mind how very little can be achieved in an hour even with the expertise of an adult! It is unlikely that first or second-year pupils will have much time in lessons as they will be doing practical work. The topic chosen must reflect the time available.

Older pupils may be able to do a project as homework and some classwork over a few weeks and can tackle longer topics but, again, these must be finite and relate realistically to the time available. Short topics might include finding specific information on one type of animal, on finding the uses of one chemical. Long topics could include water, air, the uses of a principle in physics.

3 *Direction as to the content and the level of detail required* helps the pupil over the very difficult hurdle of 'Where do I start?', 'What should I do?' The directions should not be so detailed as to become almost a worksheet but guidelines (as in essays in O and A level) that break up the topic into subsections and tell the pupil what is and is not required.

4 *Advice on where the information can be found* is helpful. The textbook will be a likely source in fourth year and above, but often in the lower school there is no textbook, or if there is a textbook it may be too brief or too practical to be useful. Pupils should be told if their own notes are a useful source of information (very often pupils totally neglect this). The fewer the sources recommended the easier the task of finding information.

5 *Information sources are reliable and accessible.* If the teacher knows that the information is adequate and easily accessible this can save much frustration on the part of the pupil. (In *Information Skills in the Secondary Curriculum* (17) one assignment is quoted on 'How was oil formed in the earth?' This ostensibly appears closed, simple, with good sources—however, the encyclopedia index volume lists 26 main entries for oil, from oil-bird to oil well, but the first entry OIL is in fact a reference to other parts of the index column. The list of terms in the index which contain the word 'oil' is almost six inches long and contains 224 words, including several unfamiliar word abbreviations, e.g. fol., bot., min., chem. Only three entries lead to the correct index term, PETROLEUM and so the tale continues. It is very doubtful if many of the first-year pupils completed this task successfully.)

Projects should develop from those needing one or two books to those requiring very wide-reaching searches.

6 *Written information is generally easier to access than non-written information.* Books are much more available than film, audio, or video cassettes. This may not be so in the future but in most schools at the moment getting access to the video tape is rather harder than burgling Fort Knox.

7 *Information can be used irrespective of its date*—the most recent developments are not required. Science books can date very quickly, units and their definitions often betray an old-fashioned

book. (It would be hoped that in a perfect library there would be very few out-of-date books but some old books can have other virtues.) Finding out the very recent developments in science requires searching in periodicals such as *New Scientist*—this is a much harder task than looking in books and can only really be expected of the sixth former.

8 *Only 'accepted wisdom' is required.* Much information in many of the societal aspects of science is highly controversial with conflicting sources and a large amount of bias. This makes selection of source and balancing of these sources a very important part of information collection. This should be part of the development of all pupils but would need to be left until the later years. Projects devoted to the more factual aspects of science will not pose these problems until pupils reach A level standard.

9 *The form of presentation is given*—whether notes, diagrams, flow-charts, essay (intro, three paragraphs, and close), etc. This simplifies the planning of the written record.

10 *Direct descriptions* only are required. It is much easier to describe than to compare and contrast, to refute or to debate. Also *chronological ordering* and *sequencing* (as in the periodic table) are much easier forms to use as plans than those that involve value judgements and balancing. Hierarchical plans are also extremely hard for pupils to devise.

All these factors make the project easier. It is not possible to develop project-writing skills one at a time. Many skills are required simultaneously but it can help if one aspect is highlighted, for example collecting information that is acceptable as jottings, whereas in another project the information is readily accessible but the method of presentation will be considered to be more important.

Here are three examples of projects ranging from the extremely simple to the very complex.

The Fins of a Fish
1 Find a diagram of a fish with all its fins labelled.
2 Find out what each fin is used for.
3 Copy the diagram and label the fins.
4 Beside each fin write down what the fin is used for.
1 week's homework—40 minutes.

This assignment requires information skills—the pupils will have to use library skills (possibly), book skills (it is not in their textbook), contents/index, skim and scanning skills. However, once the information is found the presentation is very straightforward.

> **The Life of Marie Curie**
> Find out: when she lived, how she died, her two main discoveries.
> Why are these discoveries important to us today?
>
> 1 week's homework—about 1 hour.
> You can write this as a letter, story or as a report for the school
> science magazine if you wish.

There were no books in the laboratory that would adequately cover this—only CSE and O level textbooks so the library would have to be used. Library, book-user, and reading skills would all be needed to find the information.

Although the information on Marie Curie is closed, other information would have to be found for the second section. This would require question-formation—what to look for—then a range of information skills.

Presentation can be quite difficult. Type of writing; transactional or personal has to be decided, as has audience. Sequencing can follow the question but for the last section some hierarchical ordering is needed.

A CSE project on Plastics
The pupil is told that the project should be about twelve pages minimum, it is for the examiner to read, he or she has four weeks to complete it (mainly homework—6-8 hours). Both breadth of cover and some chemical detail are required.

This project will require all the skills needed to do assignments and can be analysed using the Information Skills in Secondary Curriculum's 9 steps (see Appendix C and 17).

QUESTION 1. *What do I need to do?*
What do I know? The pupil has already 'done' plastics in class and therefore has: made some notes on polymerization, polymerized nylon and perspex and depolymerized perspex, notes on thermoplastic and thermosoftening plastics (which he didn't understand), and some names of different plastics.

Then the pupil needs to identify what must be found out. A rough plan might include: making them, uses, more on polymerization, thermosetting, etc., and examples.

QUESTION 2. *Where do I go?*
Possibilities include: library, textbook, his own notes, books/pamphlets in lab., Shell, BP, examples from home, DT department, local shops, teacher. A starting point—own notes and books in the lab.

QUESTION 3. *How do I get the information?*
Use book-user, library-user skills to search in encyclopedias, dictionaries, shelves etc. to get books together. Ask librarian if stuck. Write to Shell, BP. Ask in shops for offcuts. Ask DT department for offcuts.

QUESTION 4. *Which resources?*
Look carefully at books in lab—some too hard, some too easy, (using cover and contents), some too old (funny names). Stuff from Shell too hard.

QUESTION 5. *Using resources*
Use contents, index, pictures to find pages of information. Skim to find right sections. Read reflectively to understand. See if he can answer the original questions, do any others arise? Put in bits of paper or make notes of position.

QUESTION 6. *What to make a search of?*
Make notes of important items under the question headings.
Scan for missing information.
Copy some tables and diagrams.
Rearrange notes.

QUESTION 7. *Have I got enough and right information?*
Would this add up to 12+ pages?
Do I understand it?
Is it detailed enough?
Are there any gaps?

QUESTION 8. *Presentation*
Must be in essay form. Formal language.
Introduction.
Sections on each of the question headings and diagrams and samples.
Rounding off section at end.

QUESTION 9. *Evaluation*
Is it OK?
What does Charlton think?
What does Miss think? (17)

Appendix A

The ideal library-user education programme?

In this model, all the attitudes, knowledge and skills are introduced during the first year. During subsequent years, these are continually reinforced and treated in a depth more appropriate to the developing learner. A piece of research (i.e. a project) requires the same range of skills and abilities irrespective of pupils' age. The difference lies in the level to which the skills are developed. This is a fundamental difference in approach and one which receives little support in the literature on user education. In practice, it means that the whole range of skills should be introduced, some being taught specifically and some diffused across the curriculum in a range of different contexts. This can only be achieved if a plan is drafted, objectives defined, and areas of responsibility marked by an overall co-ordinator, either librarian or teacher. In theory (and practice) the balance falls in favour of the chartered librarian, the person most in touch with the essential supporting artefacts—library materials.

It is suggested that the timing for adoption of any, or all, of the elements in the model would be decided by the teacher; elements (or modules) could be introduced into subject teaching as and when required.

The 'ideal' Library-user education programme?

What?	*Why?*	*How?*
Year 1		
Reading for pleasure	Bridge gap between primary and secondary schools	Story-telling; book reviews; displays; film strips.
Hobbies and interests	Need to find out.	Displays; question and answer session.
Information (Concepts, contents, control) —what is information? —how much is there? —why is it needed? —where is it found? —how is it used? —when is it used?	Place concepts, values and needs for information into the child's personal context. Place libraries into the wider frame of information sources.	Talk; practical exercises; question and answer sessions; slides; television, simulation; games; quizzes.

What?	*Why?*	*How?*
School-library learning resources —contents —arrangements —retrieval strategies	Place library into the context of the curriculum. Introduce librarian and library	Library layout chart; rules and regulations poster; Dewey chart; point of use instruction for, e.g., reference books and catalogues; question and answer sessions; talk.
Projects —arrangement —search strategies —defining topics —deciding what to find out —methods to find out —purpose and audience —presentation	Refresher on primary school work. Identify differences in secondary-school approach. Equate projects with published books, etc. Introduce citation in bibliographies.	Talk; question and answer sessions on executing projects; sources; surveys and presentation; practice; handouts; demonstrations.
Resources —who writes books? —who produces tapes, TV, slides, etc.? —why? —how? —for whom? —about what? —variety —levels.	Introduce concept of recorded knowledge and access to it. Introduce varieties of recorded knowledge presentation.	Talk; question and answer sessions; demonstations; charts.
Using books —reading strategies —clues for use —reading problems —which one is right?	Instil confidence through identifying problems and possibilities.	Talk; practice; demonstration; reading aloud; reading tests; slides or charts of book parts; presentation of information in different formats using variety of media.
Using information —notemaking —organization —presentation —use	Introduce concept of audience. Introduce basic study skills. Consideration of potential end user.	Practical exercises; question and answer sessions; slides showing presentation formats.

What?	*Why?*	*How?*
Mastering the tools	Practising library research skills. Introducing secondary services, e.g. journal indexes.	Demonstration searches based on pupils' work; role playing; practical.
Summary —revision —problems —preparation	Identify problems. Obtain feedback. Fill any gaps. Prepare for next year.	Question and answer session; test or quiz; examination of pupils' work; dialogue with staff.

To be supplemented by revision sessions in the classroom for specific subject areas, as required.

Years 2 to 4
Reminders of aids.
Repeats of certain sessions to refresh memories, as required.
More details as required, noted from final evaluation session at end of first year.
Specific information searches.
Practice.
Special refreshers for fourth-year pupils.
Summary and evaluation sessions at end of each year.

Year 5
Refresher session
Emphasis on outside information sources (book, non-book and verbal):
(a) for work
(b) for domestic life
(c) for further education
Special types of material, e.g. periodicals, abstracts, indexes.

Year 6
Learning/study skills course refresher
—pattern of sixth-year study
—difficulties likely to be encountered (e.g. other distractions at school and home)
Refresher on reading strategies
Study and examination techniques.

(4)

Appendix B

Checklist XIII

Determining feasibility of assignments

Is this assignment educationally significant and worthy of the students attention?
There is too much needing to be taught and too much needing to be learned ever to permit or excuse the teaching of trivia such as 'What was the colour of Shakespeare's eyes?' Nor is there even an excuse for misleading assignments such as requiring students to locate on a world map the 'Islets of Langerhans' (endocrine glands) or including in a unit on sheep ranching the topic 'steel wool'.

Is this assignment designed to create and sustain interest in learning?
A reasonable, significant, interesting assignment that can be translated readily into foreseeable patterns of action is a strong motivational factor. Seeing purpose and promise of achievement in an assignment are powerful interest sustainers.

Is this assignment an out-growth of the unit goals and objectives?
Relevance of assignments to unit goals and objectives keeps learning activities congruent with the purpose and design of the unit. Peripheral topic inclusion not only dissipates time and energy but dissipates student interest as well.

Is this assignment essential and timely to the task at hand?
Recency, frequency, and utility are important factors in encouraging learning. It is poor teaching technique to make any assignment whose significance or relevance is not readily perceived by the student. It is an exercise in total frustration if the student does not perceive clearly the utility and the relevance of an assigned task. Idea linkage is impossible if the first link in the chain of understanding is missing.

Is this assignment suitable to the maturity level of the students?
Utter confusion arises when an assignment demands background experience or mental sophistication beyond the years the students have lived. A sense of bewilderment overwhelms any student, even the most gifted, when an assignment is incomprehensible. Who could defend assigning a third grader the research topic, 'Discuss the separation of church and state'?

Is this assignment reasonable and justifiable in the light of both time and effort required?
Nothing is more damaging to student receptivity to learning than to have an unreasonable time limitation imposed when he is being assigned a significant learning task. This is an example of interest 'overkill'. If the task is worth doing, a reasonable amount of time must be allotted for the completion of the task.

Is this assignment differentiated to meet adequately the varying capabilities of the class?
Since each student is a unique learner, mass assignments are unrealistic and pedagogically indefensible. What is a challenge and a satisfaction to one student may well be a frustrating, dead-end experience to another. How could all students in a tenth grade world history class where reading abilities range from fifth to twelfth grade be expected to read with understanding Machiavelli's *The Prince?*

Is this assignment humane in the light of the student's cultural, social, economic, and personal backgrounds?
In the scheme of teaching no phase of responsibility requires greater sensitivity on the part of the teacher than sensing what is *not* appropriate for any given class, group, or individual. Who could excuse a teacher's assigning as a topic for class discussion, 'What I got for Christmas,' when he knows that some students received nothing? In this realm alone if in no other the teacher will not be replaced by the machine, for in this area the teacher must think with his heart as well as with his mind!

Is this assignment defensible in the light of the ready availability of appropriate supporting resources in sufficient quantity?
The teacher breaks faith with the student when he bases an assignment on *too little available material or on non-existent material.* There is nothing more destructive of student interest than to be given an impossible task. Assignments requiring supporting resources that are not available readily cannot be justified by any teacher. A teacher who is the least bit introspective can well understand the negative effect of impossible assignments if he will but recall his own frustrations and feeling of resentment when as a student he was given an impossible assignment or a meaningless task. The burden of proof in finding required support materials should rest with the teacher, not with the student.

Is the assignment stated clearly so it can be translated easily into action patterns and learning strategies?
Even the most gifted and avid learner loses interest when he cannot translate an assignment into specific avenues to be followed in building and communicating understanding. Impossible assignments like 'Trace the historic development and impact of man's capacity to think individually and collectively throughout the history of mankind' or 'Write a documented research paper on the sociological, political, and anthropological aspects of the Caribbean lands' never can be completed. The student is never able to proceed past the assignment itself.

Is the assignment dependent on the utilization of new learning skills, new reference tools and techniques?
The teacher has the obligation to foresee the skills necessary for the completion of an assigned task. A competent teacher plans to equip the students to work intelligently and efficiently by introducing or having the

librarian introduce the skills and techniques essential to building the level of skill performance demanded by each assignment.

Appendix C

The nine question steps for research

1 WHAT do I need to do?
   (formulate and analyse need)
2 WHERE could I go?
   (identify and appraise likely source)
3 HOW do I get to the information?
   (trace and locate individual resources)
4 WHICH resources shall I use?
   (examine, select and reject individual resources)
5 HOW shall I use the resources?
   (interrogate resources)
6 WHAT should I make a record of?
   (record and store information)
7 HAVE I got the information I need?
   (interpret, analyse, synthesize, evaluate)
8 HOW should I present it?
   (present, communicate)
9 WHAT have I achieved?
   (evaluate)

(17)

References

1 Brake T. *The Need to know* (British Library Research and Development Report No. 5511, 1980)
2 Hanson C.S. *Research on user's needs: where is it getting us?* (ASLIB processes pp. 64–78, 1964)
3 Kelly A. *The Missing Half* (Manchester University Press 1981)
4 Irving A. and Snape W.H. *Educating Library users in secondary schools* (British Library Research and Development project 5467, 1979)
5 Department of Education and Science *Aspects of secondary education in England* (HMSO 1979)
6 Crane C. and Johnson N. Project grids *Project Grids in the School Librarian* Vol. 27 No. 3, 1979
7 Denny R.C. *Key Definitions in Chemistry* (Frederick Muller 1982)
8 Marland M. *Language across the curriculum* (Heinemann Educational Books, 1977)
9 Eggleston J. *The drawbacks of projects (Times Educational Supplement)*
10 Examples of sheets taken from Hounsell D. and Martin E. *Information Skills in the Secondary School: Teaching Resources Folder* (Lancaster: Centre for Educational Research and Development 1981. The folder was prepared as part of the project funded by The British Library Research and Development Department)
11 Ewington E.J. and Spencer J. *Projects in Biology* (Routledge & Kegan Paul 1981)
12 Mackean D. *An Introduction to Biology* (Murray 1973)
13 Cheston M. *Looking After Yourself* (Wheaton 1979)
14 Clyne S., Williams D.J.W., Clarke J.S. *A New Chemistry* (Hodder and Stoughton 1971)
15 Healy M. *Your Language Book 2* (Macmillan 1981)
16 Davies A. *The School Library, a force for educational excellence* (Bowker 1969)
17 Marland M. (ed.) *Information skills in the secondary curriculum* Schools Council Curriculum Bulletin 9, 1981.

9 Revision and examination techniques

Introduction

Until the recent development of interest in how pupils learn, for many teachers study skills and revision were almost synonymous. Study skills now encompass a much wider field than just revision skills but techniques for revising still need to be taught. Revision involves a particular set of learning tasks, very different from the research and language activities described elsewhere in this book, and as such requires special skills. Examinations likewise can be seen as special types of assignment with their own techniques.

The typical traditional teacher has always stressed the importance of examinations and has given valuable training to his or her candidates. More progressive teachers have often resented examinations as an imposition that interferes with 'real' learning, and have perhaps sometimes ignored the teaching of skills and attitudes that are exclusively geared to examinations. Very few people, however well-qualified, can look forward to revision and examinations yet it would be quite wrong, given the present emphasis on qualifications, not to train our pupils and insist that they do revise and practice their exam techniques.

Revision

1 Advice to pupils

Advice on how to revise is fraught with danger as it is an extremely idiosyncratic activity. Some people can be successful by gently sifting through Gray's anatomy (six inches thick), some make elaborate card indexes, others stick to notes and lists. There are many books on how to revise. However:

'The guides in fact provide a considerable amount of advice for pupils on how to improve. Unfortunately, not all that advice is reliable. Some is conflicting and a lot lack research evidence to support it. One reviewer has written that:

> Many analyses of study skills upon which a great deal of study skills training and advice has been based, are fundamentally unsound. Much advice claims a valid scientific basis which it simply does not have. Sometimes, as in the case of advice on memory, the basis is out-of-date laboratory psychology of extremely dubious relevance.... Sometimes the basis is little more than the impressive sounding claims and pseudo-scientific mumbo-jumbo.' (1, p. 9)

Advice given to pupils can always be rejected by them and, providing the pupils are given a variety of methods of revising, the hints and tips given by an experienced learner/teacher may be very valuable. It would neither be helpful to ignore teaching skills related to revision and examinations nor to teach one single rigid method that the pupils may well reject.

(a) Organization of time

Usually a revision programme should start five or six weeks before the examination. Pupils should be encouraged to work out a revision timetable, after answering these three questions:

1 How much time was there left for revision?
2 How much time should be spent on revising?
3 What was to be revised in each subject and in what order?
(1, p. 43)

A timetable should involve blocks of time allocated to each subject spread through the week. The balance of time given to each subject should reflect the importance, difficulty, and amount to be learnt in each subject. I always recommend three phases:

1 a thorough going-through to organize, understand and read,
2 a second phase for learning, underlining, making lists, memorizing, and
3 in the last few days a quick going-over.

The most effective time of day for learning varies. However, many pupils do completely exhaust themselves by working in the middle of the night (so much so that they have been known to be late or even miss their exam!). A definite time for starting helps a pupil to get going (which is the hardest part). I always advise pupils to start early and finish early, so that the anticipation of the revision is cut down and after it is over one can genuinely relax. It is important to give oneself little rewards after a successful bout of revision; a cup of coffee, a biscuit, a TV programme to look forward to. A deadline for finishing also acts as a very powerful goal. 'Only two hours to go' etc. makes the task seem more finite and therefore more endurable.

For younger pupils studying for exams only a short time need be set aside for revision, half-an-hour to an hour, and this should be increased to about two hours in the fourth and fifth. This time must be in half-an-hour bursts to avoid loss of concentration.

(b) Where to study

As concentration is essential and easily lost, the place where a pupil studies should be quiet and free from TV, records, family, and peers. Many sixth form common rooms are not suitable places for study, and libraries (which are often slightly better) are also likely to become overcrowded and therefore quite noisy. Schools need to look very carefully at their provision for pupils who are revising; it is not fair to require a pupil to come into school for one hour or so of good tuition amongst two or three hours that they are likely to waste chatting to friends or being disturbed.

Starting to revise needs a lot of willpower so a pupil should have a study area that is organized for revision so that time need not be spent on rearrangements. (The ritual organizing of pencils, rulers, and paper can put off the evil moment quite long enough.)

Public examinations are usually in gorgeous weather, but it is very hard to revise successfully outside—it is not comfortable and provides too many distractions.

(c) Maintaining concentration

It is only too easy for pupils to think that one is revising when in fact one is daydreaming. Pupils should be encouraged to make revision an active occupation, to:
make notes, write something (especially at the beginning), underline, make lists.

They must avoid distractions, work for only 20–40 minutes then take a definite break, when bored walkabout or change the activity and not work in a warm, drowsy place.

(d) How to give advice to pupils

Some courses provided excellent student handbooks that include advice on how to revise. (Appil, the A level physics course for example (2).)

Many schools and colleges produce leaflets or pamphlets for their pupils which are then talked through by the subject teachers or class tutors. The pastoral programme is an ideal place to deal with revision techniques as virtually all pupils in the class will be taking exams and there is time enough to hold discussions.

As much revision will be done at home, parents can be very useful in insisting that pupils do revise. It would not be wise to give parents too rigid ideas on methods of revision as they might be tempted to force their child into an ill-fitting pattern of work. However, a talk about different ways of revising and certainly guidelines on the organization of time and place of study would be very helpful. Although some pupils may wish to revise spontaneously, for the vast majority an element of coercion may well be necessary!

2 The responsibilities of the teacher

I believe that every pupil has a right to have a copy of the syllabus of their course. At the beginning of an examination course this may seem too daunting and off-putting (and unintelligible) to be helpful, but certainly halfway through a course I think it gives pupils confidence in that much has already been covered and a sense of urgency in that much still remains. Syllabuses help to put subjects into perspective, pupils can see the organization underlying the course, and can see the content on which their examination will be based. The syllabus can act as a checklist for revision and of progress. Teachers who are working too slowly will be forced to speed up by the demands of their pupils.

About halfway through an examination course I give out to the pupils booklets of past examination papers. Examination papers are written in a form of English that is very off-putting and pupils need time to familiarize themselves with their format and style. Essay-writing skills and analysis of project requirements will be very helpful. By the end of a course I think pupils should have done virtually all the old examination questions: for homework, in class, as tests and examinations.

The syllabus and examination papers together should demonstrate to pupil and teacher what is important to learn (and also that the questions are *not* predictable). The importance of some information in terms of key understanding or of examination frequency should be stressed by the teacher during teaching. (I always ask my pupils to put 'VIP Ex.' by items I know come up very frequently.) An analysis of frequency of examination questions by topics also show areas that should be emphasized (see Appendix, p. 190). Each year the examination boards write lengthy and very helpful reports on the previous examination. It is vital that all teachers of examination classes read these reports and pass on this information to their candidates. For inexperienced teachers the correct answers to multiple-choice questions, calculations, and essay plans are very useful, especially for A level. Some teacher's centres run excellent seminars that go through the recent examination which is stimulating and enlightening for all teachers. It would seem self-evident that all teachers teaching an examination course can do the examination itself but there is often discussion over the right multiple-choice question answer even among the most experienced. (It is sadly true that the *more* one knows the harder multiple-choice questions can become.) It is also very useful for young teachers to see how marks are allocated in essays. Throughout any science course it is important to test the pupils on their understanding of concepts and mastery of skills through tests or examinations. The main importance of tests lies in their diagnostic function and this is best discovered not only through using standard questions on recall but also by asking for more open-ended descriptions. Study skills covered in the course should be tested in the same way as other skills and concepts.

Examinations are usually longer than tests, and are taken under much more stringent conditions. Although an important function of a test is diagnosis, examinations are useful in assessing the progress of individuals in comparison with their peers and also to give pupils practice in sitting examinations. Providing examination practice is essential and as there are many skills associated with revision and examination technique this should not be left until the fourth or fifth year when there will not be enough time.

All examinations should be as correct and as clear in their presentation as possible. (See the checklist on writing worksheets, p. 100.) There can be few things more annoying than a RE teacher supervising a science paper with a hundred pupils in a gym with page 3 missing! The reading age of the questions should be below that of the pupils.

All examinations set should contain different elements that test different types of response, and reflect the likely final public examination. It is not very good practice to have only multiple-choice questions—despite the ease of marking. Questions should allow scope for pupils to demonstrate their study skills—essays, open-ended questions, and comprehension passages.

Some teachers may feel that giving pupils examinations is a serious restriction on their teaching. I would not agree. The examination must be based on the concepts, facts, and skills the teacher hopes the pupils have acquired. The unpleasant grind of going over their work may well help a deeper understanding to grow and also the perception of the subject as a whole to develop. As competitive examinations will have to be faced by the pupils sooner or later they must be given the practice and skills to help them to be successful.

Examination technique

Most of the more frightening aspects of examinations can be overcome by familiarity. Candidates who are used to the appearance of papers, know which paper follows which, the style of the questions, what is compulsory and what is not, will have reduced enormously the initial panic.

'There is a good deal of evidence that candidates are either not reading or are ignoring the rubric on the front of the paper.

'The most common rubric offence is for answers to be given to more than the required number of questions. This occurs in only a few instances, usually with very weak candidates and, whilst not wishing to bind themselves to a firm policy, examiners do nevertheless take the charitable view and select the best answers—more often than not to little avail!'

(3, p. 87–101)

As pupils often do not read the rubric at the front of the examination paper their teachers must ensure that they are well trained to read everything carefully and are also well-briefed as a safeguard. Exercises with mock exam instructions can be set as comprehension exercises so the implications of 'In section B candidates must answer four questions only' are really clear. Misreading or not reading the question is one of the commonest causes of candidates doing badly.

'In all questions of course candidates must expect that full credit will only be given if the question posed is answered!'
'The best advice still to most candidates is: *read the question*. This applies not only to the usual *name/formula* and see/theoretical *discussion* dichotomies but to actually *reading the whole of the question....* Candidates would do far better if they read the question, thought about it and 'roughed out' an answer plan.' (3, p. 87–101)

This exhortation to read the question is not as straightforward as it sounds, and especially with essay questions may require all of the interpretative and analytic skills. Not only is it difficult for pupils to grasp what content the question requires but they must also be aware of the structure and emphasis required. In examinations various key words are used that will determine the structure of the answer and if these key words are not recognized the answer will not be sufficient. Ann Irving has identified some of these operative words that must be understood by candidates.

DEFINE Write a concise, clear, authoritative meaning which clearly differentiates what you are defining from everything else.

COMPARE Examine qualities or characteristics to show resemblances or similarities.

CONTRAST Stress the differences between the things you are asked to contrast.

OUTLINE Develop an organized description, giving main points and essential supplementary material.

ANALYSE Show the nature of the parts and their relationships to each other, and to the whole.

EXPLAIN State the how and why, reconciling any differences in opinion, and stating causes where possible.

COMMENT Analyse and describe in a critical way showing your understanding of the different viewpoints, and what you think of them.

DISCUSS Examine the topic by arguing both or all sides, showing your grasp of the overall picture. (4)

Candidates must be given a lot of practice in writing essays with different structures according to these operative words. However, many candidates lose marks by not following the simplest of instructions:—

'It should be made clear that if a name is asked for then a name is expected.' (3)

Teachers can help train their pupils by extremely strict marking of all tests and examination questions. The initial resentment soon passes and pupils rarely persist in obvious mistakes.

How many of us have had pupils who have ruined their chances of success through bad timing? However much this is drilled into pupils they still persist. Constant practice of timed essays and doing whole papers may help, as does the instruction to divide up the time for each essay before the examination has even begun, to write it down, and to keep to it. Time can be used to help candidates. In multiple-choice question papers it is sound advice to tell pupils to mark out the answer with:—

$\times$ for incorrect
$\sqrt{}$ for correct
? can't decide

and then to leave that question until the whole paper has been completed. Very often when the candidate returns to the answer it is now obvious. (If it is not then they should again continue to the end of the paper completing all those that he or she can do and then start again. At the very end fill in *one* letter only (as this gives a 1 in 5 chance of being correct).

Choosing questions can be very difficult especially in CSE examinations where the paper can be as much as thirty pages long. The best advice is to start with the question one is most confident about and work through to the most difficult. Questions with more than one part are far easier to answer than the 'Discuss the chemistry of nitrogen in organic compounds' which requires very advanced planning skills.

'Examiners often have the impression that a multi-part question is set aside by the candidate, when one part is unfamiliar, in favour of a broader more discursive question, when perhaps unconsciously greater areas of the topic are left untouched. Unhappily, weaker candidates often choose the more demanding questions!' (3)

Other clues to the complexity of the answer required are also frequently ignored by candidates.

'Although careful thought is given to the amount of space allowed for each answer, the spaces provided will inevitably be too small for some candidates, and examiners expect, and do not penalise, an overflow into the margins or blank spaces. However, too many candidates do not take the size of the spaces provided as any guidance of what is required and thereby write long and irrelevant answers.' (3)

Or write too little in response.

Unfortunately, although in numerical answers credit is given for the working shown for the question (and therefore it must be included and not done on a desk or a scrap of paper and thrown away) even if the answer is wrong there is no credit given for an essay plan. This is unfortunate as it is the drawing up of a plan that is the really difficult intellectual task—as can be seen in Chapter 8 *Information skills.*

More and more frequently examination boards are including continuous assessment, course work, and projects as part of the assessment. This new emphasis must increase the importance of work on study skills rather than revision skills and examination technique. As pupils are having to work independently for long periods during their course, and have the time and lack of stress to produce their best, this new development is to be very warmly welcomed.

Appendix

Questions set on ILPAC topics 1–4 between 1972–79

1 Amount of substance		3 Gases	
Jan '72	3	Specimen paper	7
Jan '73	1	Jan '73	8
Jan '74	6	Jun '73	6
Jan '75	1	Jun '74	5
Jan '77	6	Jan '77	4
		Jun '79	1

2 periodic table		4 Atoms	
Specimen paper	1	Jun '72	8
Jan '72	1	Jan '73	4
Jan '73	5	Jan '74	6
Jun '73	1	Jun '73	5
Jan '74	8	Jan '74	1
Jan '74	6	Jan '75	1
Jun '74	1	Jan '76	1
Jun '74	6	Jun '76	1
Jun '74	7	Jan '77	1
Jan '75	6	Jun '77	1
Jun '75	7	Jun '77	7
Jun '76	4	Jun '78	4
Jan '78	3	Jun '78	1
Jan '78	7	Jun '79	7
Jun '78	4	Jun '79	1
Jun '79	1		
Jun '79	3		
Jun '79	2		
☐ Essay			

References

1 Irving A. *Starting to teach study skills* (Edward Arnold 1982)
2 Bailson, J., Covell, A, Davies, D, Beckett, L. *Appil Students' Handbook* (Learning Materials Service, ILEA 1976)
3 London University Examination Board *Examiners report* (London University 1981)
4 Irving, A. *Study Skills across the Curriculum* (Heinemann Educational Books, *Organisation in Schools* series 1983).

10 Teaching language and study skills in science

Introduction

There can be no doubt that pupils will benefit immensely if their school has a co-ordinated policy across the whole curriculum for the teaching of language and study skills. Language skills cross all subject boundaries as reading, writing, talking, and listening skills are common to virtually every discipline. Study skills—which are essentially the skills needed for pupils to become independent learners—should also cross most subject boundaries. The identification of information required, how to find, record, communicate, and evaluate information are essential skills throughout the academic curriculum as are organization skills and learning how to learn.

Each skill requires an initial teaching session that is devoted to explanation and simple practice. As this is very time-consuming this training should not be confined to a subject such as science that has many other unique aims. Ideally many of the skills should be introduced in English lessons or as part of a pastoral programme and then reinforced and practised immediately in as many other subjects as possible. This implies a very clear language policy both in terms of well-defined aims and objectives and a temporal framework.

Sadly in the eight years since the publication of the Bullock report there has not been very much progress towards this ideal.

'Language across the curriculum policies are hard to achieve and have not been devised in the majority of schools and implemented in far fewer.'

(1, p. 102–86)

This chapter hopes to give some advice on how language and study skills can be fitted into a science lesson—either as part of a cross-curriculum policy or if there is no school-wide policy just within a science department. Hopefully successful practice within the science department might encourage other departments to follow suit and achieve by piecemeal methods a whole-school policy.

Teaching language and study skills is not an easy training process. Use of these techniques cannot be taught once and for all, unlike the use of a burette for example. The introduction of the skill has to be followed by practice, the development of learning habits and attitudes. Ralph Tabberer in Ann Irving's book on study skills says this very clearly:

'Planning study skills teaching should ... mean planning the teaching of study habits. It is not as easy, however, to inculcate or change a habit as it is to demonstrate a technique ... Pupils may know about skills and techniques and not use them'. (2, p. 11)

After instruction and simple exercises using the new skill, the study skills programme must continue with more practice within a widening variety of contexts, and reinforcement and sophistication of the technique through a variety of different assignments. Opportunities for pupils to use the technique should be created and not bypassed. The developing of these habits by the pupils will not be possible unless the pupil has a positive attitude to her or his own learning. The doling out of study skill exercises will not result in the pupil becoming an autonomous learner—the atmosphere within the laboratory or classroom has to encourage independence and self-reliance so that study skills become essential learning tools and are practised continually and spontaneously. Only when there is the right atmosphere can the pupils attitude promote within themselves good learning habits.

The teaching methods used in many secondary schools are very different from the methods used both in universities and primary schools. University courses have always used a great diversity of teaching methods and required their pupils to be independent learners and to possess advanced study skills. Primary schools nowadays also see their pupils as independent learners and the wide variety of activities happening happily and purposefully in a primary classroom puts many a secondary school to shame. Pupils, when they arrive at a secondary school, use many basic study skills, many have done projects that require finding out information and making notes—and yet rather than develop these skills in secondary schools they are often ignored until the fourth or fifth years by which time they have atrophied.

There should be a continuous progression in pupils' education from dependence to independence in learning so that by the time pupils leave school they can function as autonomous learners. They will need such skills in order to become independent.

Altering one's own teaching style may appear formidable, too daunting to contemplate, but changes do not have to be total or even very radical to be worthwhile. Changing from note-taking to note-making, changing the style of practical writing-up and other simple alterations will have very positive results in improving pupils' learning.

Many teachers now have to teach mixed ability groups. If classes are grouped in mixed abilities (and even setted or streamed classes have pupils of different abilities) then some differentiation of work will be essential. Work on study skills can only help the teacher provide for the more and less able simultaneously by giving pupils the skills to work on their own.

Problems

1 *When to introduce study skills*

If study skills are timetabled as a separate lesson there will be some reluctance to give up subject teaching time, but this may seem the easiest solution as it avoids the need for inter-departmental communication and departmental autonomy is maintained. However, unless study and langauge skills are practised within other subjects then timetabled lessons will fail in their purpose and be seriously undervalued by the pupils who will not see how to transfer their skills into real learning. Whether there is a separate lesson called 'study skills' or not there must be a policy across departments that will demand interdepartmental co-operation and loss of some autonomy.

Study skills programmes are being introduced into some sixth form courses, often as part of an induction programme, separate from the academic subjects. Not only does this approach leave out completely the 50% of the population who leave school before the sixth form and avoid any departmental involvement, but also can be counterproductive for the sixth formers themselves. By the sixth form pupils will have already formed their own study habits (and these can be quite bizarre, time-consuming, and inefficient) and 'many who have tried to introduce pupils to new techniques have mentioned the difficulty of persuading pupils, especially older ones, to change the ways they work' (2). Pupils themselves find that a conflict between new techniques of learning and their own established pattern of work very unsettling.

It is not really possible to start teaching study skills in the fourth and fifth year when the examination pressure is extremely great. Usually pupils have a wide variety of option subjects to choose from, and although these subjects can help reinforce and utilize study skills it is only the common core subjects (such as English) that could be used for initial training. This would place an enormous burden on one department which is, as are all the others, working towards an examination.

Study and language skills should be taught in the first year of secondary schooling. The initial training in each skill is best done during timetabled English lessons and during the pastoral programme and then practised in other subjects. Elementary skills and methods of working learnt in the primary school can be continued, augmented, and refined. An early start will avoid bad habits developing, and the possibility of conflict between techniques. As most first year groupings are mixed ability then these skills need to be developed in the first year so that the pupils can work more independently.

In the early years of secondary schooling the pupils' cognitive development will not be sufficiently advanced for the most sophisticated use of skills, as are needed in lengthy essays and project assignments, but should be adequate for making notes, using the simple DARTS, taking part in discussion, etc.

2 Mixed ability classes

Mixed ability grouping of pupils is extremely popular in many schools. An HMI survey of mixed ability schools in 1976 showed that:

> most subjects mixed ability Year 1–5   2%
> most subjects mixed ability Year 1–3   9%
> most subjects mixed ability Year 1–2 12%
> most subjects mixed ability Year 1   <u>12%</u>
>   35%   (3, p. 11)

However the same survey concluded over and over again that:

'(The) Same basic content is offered to all ... the choice of material being determined by the needs of the large middle range of pupils. As a result there was often inadequate differentiation to meet the requirements of pupils of markedly differing abilities'.   (3, p. 35)

Independent learning was not being used successfully:

'In some cases the pupils experience was widened by individual learning based on the use of prepared resources ... But in methods of motivation, pace, levels of difficulty and academic challenge, the hope underlying resource-based methods had not often been realised. Sometimes resources were simply insufficient or unsuitable.'   (3, p. 37)
'Some teaching methods when used to excess produced boredom. Work-sheets especially were not popular with pupils.'   (3, p. 44)

The problems of the gifted or more able pupil was felt to be especially acute in mixed ability classes.

'—it (mixed-ability grouping) had led to an extension of the range of content for pupils in the lower ability range: but it had often produced some restriction of experience for the most able which could lead to serious under-achievement.'   (3, p. 57)
'Work for the more able was often repetitions of the same or unnecessary reinforcement of work already understood.'   (3, p. 134)

This report on mixed ability teaching echoed an earlier report on Gifted Children in Middle and Comprehensive Secondary Schools.

'Science teachers are generally aware of the gifted but have few solutions about how to provide for them.'   (4, p. 94)

This report was particularly scathing about homework.

'We found few cases where a teacher had given homework intended to differentiate between various ability levels ... one task was given to all pupils in a class or set. Undifferentiated homework tasks usually reflected undifferentiated classroom teaching.'   (4, p. 30)

The problems of providing adequate educational diets are not just confined to the 'understretched' more able pupil. The HMI secondary survey was also worried about provision in mixed ability classes for the less able.

'In at least a quarter of the schools it was the least able who suffered particularly from a failure to extend their reading or to provide an appropriate range of materials.'   (1, p. 74)

The difference in development between the more able and the less able within a mixed ability group can be quite enormous. Shayer found in his study of pupils' cognitive development in science that there could be as much as nine years difference between the most and least able third year pupils.

	Bottom			*Top*	
Percentiles of population	0 - 20%	- 50%	- 80%	- 95% +	
Difference in development		3 years	3 years	3 years	(5, pp. 45, 131)

Any teacher would have grave difficulties in coping with pupils of such diversity but many mixed ability classes and even streamed classes must contain pupils whose developmental stages are many years apart.

'To deal with these extremes and the wide spectrum between them in one group so as to provide for their several and widely different needs demands exceptional professional qualities. HM Inspectors saw a number of teachers of high quality who handled mixed ability groups with great skill and enterprise, so that the able were extended, the average and below average were lifted in aspiration and achievement, and the less able were encouraged, helped, and given pride in achievement and motivation to progress. In the hands of the average teacher, however, the mixed ability class tended to function at the level of the average pupil. For the weaker teacher, the challenge of the mixed ability class was simply too great.' (3, p. 53)

3 Girls

Approximately half the pupils in secondary schools are girls and yet the percentage of girls choosing the physical science in the fourth/fifth year is very much less than the percentage of boys.

Table 1.1 The percentage of girls and boys being offered, taking and obtaining qualifications in science subjects in the last years of compulsory schooling

	(a) *Being offered (% of fourth and fifth form pupils)*	(b) *Choosing (% of col. (a))*	(c) *Taking (% of fourth and fifth form pupils*	(d) *Attempting CSE or O level (% of 1975–76 school leavers)*	(e) *Passing O level* (% of 1975–76 school leavers)*
Physics					
Girls	71	17	12	9	5
Boys	90	52	47	40	16
Chemistry					
Girls	76	22	17	12	6
Boys	79	35	27	25	12
Biology					
Girls	95	52	49	46	18
Boys	88	31	28	27	12
Maths					
Girls	n.d.	n.d.	n.d.	68	20
Boys	n.d.	n.d.	n.d.	70	27

Note n.d. = no data
*Grades A–C and CSE Grade 1
Source. (a), (b), (c), Department of Education and Science, Curricular Differences for Boys and Girls, Education Survey 21, table 6, HMSO, 1975; (d), (e) Department of Education and Science, Statistics of Education, 1976, Vol. 2, table 8, HMSO, 1977. (6, p. 3)

This problem has been widely investigated and one finding that is pertinent to study skills and language has been identified by Alison Kelly.

'As one goes up the qualification ladder in science a smaller and smaller percentage of women succeed.'   (6, p. 5)

'Girls, on average, have greater verbal skills than boys, and they frequently perform better in written work. But this aspect of science tends to be devalued by comparison with mathematical and theoretical approaches.'
(6, p. 278)

There are immense differences between the biological and physical sciences. One of these is that biology as a school subject concentrates much more on verbal skills—perhaps this is one aspect that attracts girls to this subject.

Teacher's attitudes towards expectations of girls is significantly different from their attitude and expectation of boys. Teacher questions to the class are particularly prone to sex bias.

Girls also enjoy using their imagination especially in social or personal contexts—this is usually disregarded in science lessons—but need not be if teachers encouraged a much broader range of writing styles and contexts.

In many science examinations at 16+ it is the multiple-choice questions and short-answer questions that make up the majority of the marks. This favours the boys who do well in these types of text and does not favour the girls who are better at essays.

Girls are likely to be successful learners of language and study skills and if they were introduced to science lessons it may result in girls enjoying and being more successful at learning science itself. The atmosphere within a lesson where pupils are more independent learners is more likely to appeal to the girls than a very teacher-dominated lesson.

Strategies

1 Science department policy

Ideally there should be a whole-school policy for language and study skills. If a school has such a policy then every department, including science, will have to translate that policy into a programme that is included in the departmental scheme of work. If there is no whole-school policy then the science department must devise its own programme although this will not be nearly as full and therefore not as successful as if all subjects were involved.

A language and study skills programme should start in the first year and follow what is called a spiral curriculum throughout the core science programme. If science is not compulsory in the fourth and fifth years then recommendations should be made so that the work covered in the early years is not forgotten even under the pressure of examination syllabuses.

A spiral programme for the teaching of study skills

This programme is an attempt to give a sequence for the teaching of study skills so that pupils move from the fundamental skills to the more complex skills and have sufficient mastery of the individual skills so that they can use them in conjunction to write essays and projects.

The programme must be a spiral so that after each skill is taught it is reinforced and elaborated in different subjects and throughout all the years.

Year 1

Reading skills

1 Reading for pleasure—continuous reading.
2 Reading to find information:
(a) underlining searching for specified targets in the text;
(b) diagram completion, pupil prediction of deleted labels and/or parts of diagrams using the text and diagrams as sources of information;
(c) completion activities with disordered text, prediction of the logical order or resequencing disordered text;
(d) prediction of next part of text;
(e) skimming;
(f) scanning.

3 Increasing the speed and fluence of reading:
(a) cloze procedures.
4 Using books:
(a) choosing the appropriate reading strategy.

Writing skills

1 Simple notemaking from one or two texts:
(a) audience largely peer;
(b) story-telling;
(c) making scripts for plays and tapes.

Talking and listening

1 Small group discussion about tasks

Information-finding

1 The concept of

information-finding
Information (concepts)
—what is information?
—how much is there?
—why is it needed?
—where is it found?
—how is it used?
—when is it used?
Layout of library
Borrowing procedures, opening hours, rules
Subject index
Catalogue of library stock
Classification scheme (Dewey)

Search terms
Alphabetical/numerical order
Shelf arrangements (fiction, non-fiction, pamphlets, oversize books, periodicals, audio-visual materials)
Finding items on shelves
Catalogues
Reference books
Encyclopedias
Dictionaries

Using books
Parts of a book
Contents pages
Index
Alphabetical order
Skimming
Scanning

Year 2

Reinforcement by repetition and development of skills learnt in year one.

Years 2 to 4

Reminders of aids.
Repeats of certain sessions to refresh memories, as required.
More details as required, noted from final evaluation session at end of first year.
Specific information searches.
Practice.
Summary and evaluation sessions at end of each year.

Reading skills

1 *Classifying* segments according to categories given by teacher

2 *Labelling*
Pupil labelling of segments of text (e.g. paragraphs) which deal with *different* aspects of text with labels provided by teachers
3 *Segmenting*
(a) Segmenting of paragraphs or text into information units.
(b) Labelling of segments of text without labels provided by teacher; producing classification for segments of text.

Writing skills

Developing different styles of note-making.

Recording

Diagrammatic representation

Constructing diagrams of content of text making a choice from flow diagrams, hierarchies, networks, or models, continua, mindmaps.

Changing audience
Variety of audience and appropriateness from peer to public. Advertisements, reports, instructions.

Projects
Developing from simple to complicated
—arrangement
—search strategies
—defining topics
—deciding what to find out
—methods to find out
—purpose and audience
—presentation.
Making video/audio tapes for different audiences.

Year 3

Reinforcement

Reading skills

1 *Table completion*
   Completion of tables, using table categories and text as sources of reference.
2 *Tabular representation*
   Pupil construction of tables from information given in text.

Writing skills

Essay writing
   planning—selection of information
   communication
   shaping
   presentation.
discussion of how to write essays.
Virtually all writing to be transactional.
Audience to become much more frequently adult/examiner.
More complex projects.
Examination technique
   answering multiple-choice questions
   structured questions.
Revision skills
   organizing time
   concentration.

Years 4–5

Much more revision.
Examination technique.

Answering complex multi-response multiple-choice questions.
Essay writing from examination papers.
Discussion—use of operative words.
Project help for CSE candidates.
Transactional mode for most writing.

Year 5

Refresher session
Emphasis on outside information sources, (book, non-book, and verbal)
(a) for work
(b) for domestic life
(c) for further education.
Special types of material, e.g. periodicals, abstracts, indexes.

Year 6

Learning/study skills course refresher
—pattern of sixth-year study
—difficulties likely to be encountered (e.g. other distractions at school and home).
Refresher on reading strategies.
Study and examination techniques.
Essays—what is required
   operative words
   discuss good and bad
   mark other pupils' work
   presentation/shape of essays.
Revision skills
Examination techniques } revision

Once an outline policy has been drawn up it is important to identify what particular concepts or practical work in science will lend itself to teaching and practising each skill. Teachers who are unfamiliar with teaching study skills will need to know exactly what is expected of them, what is available and when exercises, etc. are appropriate. Written resources such as cloze exercises, textbooks, diagrams must be in the teacher's pack and given equal status with other items such as practical and safety instructions.

Coming from different primary schools and having different abilities, pupils will have very different skills and levels of development. Therefore the resources for teaching study skills must be very varied. Fortunately the resources need not be confined to teacher-produced worksheets but could include questions that groups could discuss, writing stories or accounts, reading from reference or textbooks, finding out from the library. Any scheme of work for teachers new to this aspect of teaching should include a wide variety of hints on resources and different tasks that could be set.

In-service training for teachers within the department through the writing of materials and the drawing up of the schemes of work will be invaluable. Teachers who have been involved from the beginning of a project are much more likely to be committed to its success than those who feel a change has been imposed upon them.

'It is difficult to persuade teachers to change traditional, though not demonstrably effective, attitudes and practices.' (7, p. 23)

Contributions from other teachers and discussion of the tasks given to pupils are very important because many of the separate skills we wish to teach are bound up in our minds with very old habits and it is very difficult to dissect out the constituent skills needed to write an essay or make notes. David Martin and Paul Buck offer some sound advice to teachers beginning to teach study skills.

'You may not be really aware of the skills you are trying to teach because you apply them instinctively.

Try, therefore, to analyse, isolate and define them carefully before developing materials.

The more you analyse, the more complex the web of skills appears to be. Try to relate specific skills to specific needs over the child's school career.

You will need to convince others of the need for study skills teaching. If course materials or teaching methods higher up the school, or in the next school, do not take advantage of these newly acquired skills, then they will be largely forgotten by most of the pupils and your work will have been in vain. (The Schools Council publication *Information Skills in the Secondary Curriculum* may give you some useful ammunition.)

Involve all the relevant teaching staff in the production of materials to ensure that they are sympathetic to the course, and that they understand it themselves.' (2, p. 89)

If pupils are being taught study skills then the testing of these skills should form part of the science assessment and monitoring programme. Pupils are only too aware of the status of knowledge and if a skill or a fact is not to be tested or examined it loses status. Furthermore it is vital to assess how successful the study skills programme has been, to spot areas for improvement in the programme and to assess the progress of each pupil.

2 *When to teach study skills*

In the previous sections the reasons for starting teaching language and study skills in the first year were given with an outline programme for years one to six. Detailed schemes of work tell the teacher what resources are available and match the work in science that pupils are doing in specific topics and even lessons with appropriate language and study skills work. However there still remains the problem of when within a lesson is a suitable time to teach study skills. Some skills may have to be taught as new skills within the science lesson to all pupils. How to use an index, how to find books in the library, how to set about a new project *may* have to be taught to all pupils, or a large section of them, although, hopefully, much of this will have been covered in English or the pastoral programme. Small groups can be taught a new technique when their work makes it necessary. Discussions in groups with a teacher helping can also initiate the teaching of a new skill.

Firm guidance and instruction is needed for the younger pupil and assignments that involve new skills or a new complex series of skills. Guidance may need to be given during the first attempts and most importantly at the end of an assignment based on a new skill. Follow-up of work based on new skills is vitally important for learning and is often neglected because of the pressures of time. Apart from the time set aside for the teaching of skills, practice can be fitted into any empty slot that occurs within a lesson—for example when practical work has been finished.

'In about one third of all schools it was apparent that insufficient demands were made of able pupils. For example, those who finished practical work long before the rest of the class were frequently left with nothing to do.'   (1, p. 185)

During practical work there frequently occur hiatuses when the apparatus is being used by others, is not prepared, or breaks! Study skills tasks like cloze procedures, reading of the textbook, discussion about last week's experiment can be usefully slotted in to fill the gap. Indeed most teachers fill up these gaps already with work of this nature.

When science classes are not able to be in a laboratory, work involving the teaching and developing of study skills can be used to continue learning in science. (For one year I was not timetabled in a laboratory for a first year science lesson and we spent most of that time in the library finding out information and writing notes on animals.)

Resources geared to improving language and study skills always to hand will undoubtedly help the more able pupil by providing them with an infinite and varied series of tasks to perform. (It will also help to keep the less motivated out of mischief.) Study skills work can be very easily tailored to pupil's intellectual level and interests. Once pupils can find out things for themselves it is not too difficult for the teacher to set interesting and challenging tasks.

Extended projects that can be done in the interstices of lessons or at home provide an excellent opportunity to develop skills, maximize pupil interest and involvement. Pupils do project work in primary schools and are used to working on them when they have finished their other tasks. Obviously the level and complexity of the project will vary with the age and skill of the pupil.

Teachers of practical subjects such as science are sometimes not very skilful at setting good homework assignments because much of the work done in class does not easily lend itself to expansion or continuation at home. Many of the study skills exercises and tasks would make excellent homeworks ranging from the very simple cloze procedures, identifying information from texts and other simple DARTS, to the extended essay and project. Using language and study skills exercises it is possible to set very different homework for different pupils. (Setting homework can become very complicated and my answer has been to give all pupils the same easy homework and then to give pupils who can, or who want to do more, packs of homework either from a book with exercises, or an extended piece of work that will last 2–3 weeks thereby avoiding having to set different homeworks every lesson.)

Apart from plugging gaps in a lesson with work related to study skills, subtle changes in style of teaching can make a tremendous difference to the work done by pupils in a lesson, as can be seen in these two descriptions of lessons.

Panel 8.2 *The problem of digestion: another lesson with thirteen-year-olds.*

Four boys arrive early and nose around the demonstration bench, where there is a partially dissected rat covered by a damp cloth. They peer under the cloth and point out to each other the things they know—liver, intestines. 'Where's the kidneys?', says one. 'Are we doing this today?', says another to the teacher, who is sorting papers a few feet away. She nods and carries on with what she is doing, but after a while diverts two of the boys to write on the board a full list of what they ate for lunch. The rest arrive. The teacher points out the lists on the board, and asks

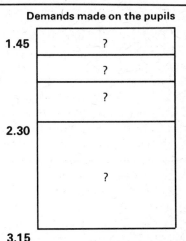

questions about what foods are for. 'For energy', 'They help you grow', and so on. She points out that although the boys' arms and legs are certainly growing they aren't actually made of lettuce and carrot, or cheese and onion pie, and poses the problem of how 'food stuff' is changed into 'body stuff', and how it gets to the parts of the body where it is needed.

1.55 After a pause she explains the idea of breaking things down, to make the materials for new constructions. She uses the analogy of house demolition to give bricks and wood and wire, etc., that might be used in a new building, lists these on the board, and then asks the class to make similar lists of the usable parts of cheese and onion pie, OR ham sandwich OR fruit cake. (One group to each food.) As they write their lists she wanders among them, and chides those girls who have listed pastry as pastry rather than fat and starch. A spokesman for one group reads out their list, and the teacher says 'Now we will go on to examine the cheese and onion pie demolishing machinery of a human being ... or at least of a rat ...' Some of the boys push John forward, saying 'He'll do, there's no difference.'

2.05 They crowd around as the rat is unveiled and the teacher quickly traces the digestive system, starting with the teeth. 'What is their part in the whole job?' For some (easy) parts she simply points with a needle and says nothing, whereupon they name them or ask questions ('How long is its intestine?'). She listens, and then offers more description and explanation. She takes a long time to explain what the pancreas does. Finally she points out the blood vessels around the gut and asks for speculation as to why there are so many, and what they are for. Several hands go up, but it's a question just to think about, and the pupils are sent back to their places to start on the following tasks. They can choose which to do first.

(i) to write down their ideas about the rich blood supply, with reasons,

(ii) to stick in their books a duplicated diagram, and to write in opposite it what happens in each section of the gut (books available),

(iii) to identify parts in a photograph of a rabbit's gut, and then draw it,

(iv) given the length of the rat, and of its intestine, to calculate a likely length of a human intestine.

2.30–3.15 Pupils writing and talking. Most complete two of them before the bell goes.

Panel 8.1 *The gut of a rat: a lesson with thirteen-year-olds.*

'Oh, sir, we've got you again have we? It's made my day', says Marion good naturedly, as she waltzes, rather conspicuously, to hang her coat on the pegs at the side of the laboratory. The teacher finds her irritating, and tells her off sharply. He takes a register, stopping several times to insist that they settle down and be quiet.

After a brief revision question to make a link with the last lesson the pupils are asked to copy a title from the board, 'Looking at the gut of a rat'. Then they gather

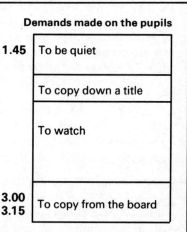

Demands made on the pupils

1.45	To be quiet
	To copy down a title
	To watch
3.00 **3.15**	To copy from the board

round to watch. The teacher has the rat and dissection tools ready. 'Now this is a deep frozen rat. Someone tell me what sex it is.' They peer over the carcass with giggles and nudges, but the animal's external anatomy is not very clear. 'Well, it's a female', he says. He starts cutting. His delivery is spontaneous and fluent. By the time he has pointed out the stomach, liver and diaphragm they have settled down and their interest is held.

Periodically there are cries of Ugh! and Uugh! One girl is upset, perhaps ready to vomit, certainly to weep. The teacher notices, and asks Marion to take her out and look after her. Marion takes her to the preparation room, where Mrs L, the laboratory steward, is working.

The teacher goes on describing the parts revealed by the dissection, going into some detail—the caecum, the mesentery. He describes their functions. A few questions are asked, mostly 'What's that?', and he answers them directly. Some of the boys break away in giggly asides and are quelled: 'Shut up while I'm talking.'

Having completed the tour of the abdomen, the teacher cuts through the ribs to show the heart, lungs and windpipe. 'Are you going to do the brain?', asks someone.

After about 35 minutes the pupils go back to their places, and copy notes from the board, followed by a diagram. They chat amongst themselves as they do so, and the teacher rebukes them periodically, urging them to 'get on with it'.

Libraries are often very popular places for pupils to congregate and look at books and periodicals. As science teachers it is very important that we ensure that the library is well-stocked with science books (including textbooks for those doing homework) that are interesting and cover a wide range of reading ages. Pupils should be introduced by their science teacher to the references and science sections in the library.

'In many schools, librarians contribute a valuable source of support for gifted children.'   (4)

3 The less able pupils

It is clear that introducing study skills work into science will benefit the more able pupils, but it is not perhaps as obvious what study skills work can offer the less able pupil.

Firstly, if teachers are aware of the importance of language and study skills then they will be aware also of the importance of getting the language levels right for all pupils. At the moment many pupils are struggling with written material (teacher-produced as well as published) that is far too difficult for them. Other pupils are suffering from not having any stimulation to read or write and their embryonic skills are not being developed. Even if these pupils do not master the multiplicity of skills needed to write essays or start projects they should be in a learning environment where they can cope and be given a structured programme to develop their reading and writing.

Many of the simple DARTs—cloze, sorting out disjointed information, filling in diagrams and tables, use of indexes, skimming and scanning—can be quite enjoyable and simple enough to be success-ful. These tasks need not take a very long time so that pace and variety can be maintained. These tasks can also be used or devised by the remedial department so that their extra help in English is related to their work in science.

An extra teacher and helper in the laboratory would be immensely valuable in developing these skills.

Pupils who have difficulty in reading and writing may develop useful and sound scientific concepts through talk and discussion. Opportunities for pupils to discuss the purpose and results of prac-tical work are very important. Working collaboratively in small groups also helps to increase understanding and communication through talk and increases helpful collaboration amongst pupils.

Appendix

Whole school policy on study skills

Contents

1 Introductory statement
2 Aims and general objectives of a study skills policy
3 A checklist of study skills
4 The implications of a whole school policy on study skills
5 Proposals
Appendix A—A study skills matrix
6 Bibliography and further reading
7 Acknowledgements

Whole school policy on study skills

1 *Introductory statement*

(i) Traditionally, education is seen as a process by which infor-mation and ideas are 'fed into' the individual from different areas of knowledge. The direction is from the subject to the individual; she/he is expected to absorb, learn, and remember as much as pos-sible. Much consideration has, correctly, been given to developing a content curriculum that is appropriate to the needs of the students and has relevance for the modern world.

In recent years there has been an increasing emphasis in schools on the process of learning. This focus on 'how children learn' rather than solely on what they learn has led to a growing demand for the teaching of study or learning skills and the enhancement of autonomous learning by pupils.

This has been reflected in new modes of examinations and in course work assessment and applies also to work of all levels and types within schools. The recent Schools Council Curriculum Bulletin No. 9, *Information Skills in Secondary Curriculum* identified areas of learning skills and strategies for teaching them in schools. Examples of these skills are:

(a) Self organization and planning
(b) Note-taking and note-making
(c) Appropriate reading strategies
(d) Library user skills
(e) Question formulating
(f) Writing for specific purpose and audience
(g) Listening skills

These skills can be taught in schools; this teaching is most effective if it is embedded into subject teaching and learning across the curriculum (including the pastoral curriculum). Experience shows that as children develop these skills, they gain more confidence and can manage their own learning since they understand the nature of the learning process. Children can work at their own pace and extend themselves as they adopt the tools to learning independently. By focussing on the process of learning, it is easier for the teachers to identify learning problems and to plan appropriate individual strategies. Pupils then find it easier to assess their own learning and to transfer learning experiences from one subject area to another.

A school policy on study skills is an attempt to develop a skills curriculum that gives the pupils increased autonomy over their learning and aims to help children to see learning as a continuous process which goes beyond their years in school.

(ii) Mixed ability teaching, now common throughout much of the school, necessitates that a large proportion of the children's time is spent working on their own tasks, either individually or in groups. However, we cannot just leave it to pupils to acquire the requisite skills for independent learning. Instead of just teaching content, we must help them to learn how to learn, think, recall, create, solve problems, and acquire the skills essential to study. They then have a direction of learning which goes out from them, the pupils to the subject.

(iii) Research has shown that an isolated study skills programme is at best ineffective, and can be confusing, if not damaging.

Isolated from the content of the curriculum, there is some danger that concentration on learning skills may be viewed as a trivial activity. Moreover, an unrelated study skills programme could define learning skills which confuse the pupils and may not answer their real learning needs. Study skills should form an integral part of the planned teaching and learning programme and should be the responsibility of all teachers.

2 *The aims and general objectives of a study skills policy*

2.1 The aims of a study skills policy should be to provide pupils with a range of skills that allow them to choose the most appropriate and personally satisfying strategies for the task in hand.

2.2 A whole school policy on study skills should aim to provide a continuity of learning experiences between departments and between subjects. The development of such a policy, as an integral part of the curriculum, will provide a unifying process whereby the pupils will be encouraged to transfer and extend skills from one area of the school curriculum to another.

2.3 By emphasizing the process of learning, as well as the content, the pupils should begin to participate in, and increasingly be responsible for their own learning. A study skills policy should aim for a decreasing dependence on the teacher so that the learners' autonomy should be complete by the end of the 6th year.

2.4 The general objectives of the policy are to articulate ways of helping students to:

(a) achieve a measure of self-organization in their work,
(b) approach a variety of learning tasks independently and effectively,
(c) handle the resources available to them with confidence,
(d) develop skills and attitudes which generate a 'need to know',
(e) communicate effectively with a sense of audience and certainty.

3 *A checklist of study skills*

This is a checklist of study skills contained in an integrated skills programme.

1 Self-organization and planning.

2 Finding information and collecting data.
3 Using books and other resources.
4 Reading skills.
5 Listening and viewing skills.
6 Speaking skills.
7 Note-making and note-taking.
8 Using information.
9 Presenting information.
10 Self-appraisal.
11 Examination techniques.

3.1 Self-organization and planning

3.1.1 *Self-organization*
defining nature, range, meaning, purpose, and direction of task relating and cross-referring, linking with what already is known and what needs to be known.
sequencing–sorting out how first to tackle the task, and what to emphasize.

3.1.2 *Planning*
planning time on a task; a project; a week's work; a term's work
organizing materials
organizing activities
monitoring the plan over time.

3.2 Finding information and collecting data

3.2.1 *Using the school and other libraries*
(a) Types of materials held
(b) Layout, procedures, rules
(c) Classification scheme
(d) Subject index
(e) Shelf arrangements
(f) Strategies for finding information
(c.f. whole school policy on Library User Education.)
Pre-requisite skills
(a) alphabetical order
(b) numerical order

3.2.2 *Making use of other agencies*
e.g. government departments

local authorities
industrial and commercial companies
service organizations
associations and societies.

3.2.3 *Collecting information from primary sources*
e.g. people
places, sites, buildings
physical and natural world.

3.2.4 *Using different methods for information and data collection*
(a) selecting
(b) reading
(c) interviewing
(d) surveying
(e) observing
(f) listening
(g) recording

3.3   Using books and other materials

3.3.1 *Using books*
(a) Types of books and other printed material
   (i) fiction
  (ii) non fiction
 (iii) reference books
       bibliographies
       dictionaries
       encyclopedias
       directories
       yearbooks
       handbooks and manuals
       atlases
       periodicals, magazines, and newspapers
(b) parts of books
    (i) titles and authors
   (ii) preface/foreword
  (iii) tables of contents
  (iv) subject index
   (v) chapter and sub-headings
  (vi) summaries and abstracts
 (vii) bibliographies and references
(viii) footnotes
  (ix) glossaries
   (x) appendices.

3.3.2 Using non-print material
   (a) tapes and casettes
   (b) records
   (c) slides, photographs, and pictures
   (d) films and filmstrips
   (e) video-tapes.

3.4 Reading skills
3.4.1 Reading for different purposes
      reading textbooks and set books
      background and general reading
      reading for literary criticism and appreciation; interpretation; analysis
      reading for pleasure.

3.4.2 Reading strategies
      e.g. S.Q. 3R, skimming; scanning; previewing and reviewing, reflective reading.
      (c.f. whole school policy on reading.)

3.5 Listening and viewing skills

3.5.1 Listening
      e.g. for fact, opinion, instruction

3.5.2 Viewing skills
      e.g. for TV, film demonstration, media-related skills.
      (c.f. whole school policy on Media Education.)

3.5.3 Interpreting illustrations
   (a) charts and diagrams
         line graphs
         bar charts
         flow charts
         pie diagrams
         spider webs
   (b) tables
         tables
         timetables
         matrices
   (c) maps, sketches, plans
         keys
         grids

colour
shape
scale
direction
projection
(d) symbols
(e) pictures and photographs
angle
lighting
accuracy
bias
(c.f. whole school policy on visual literacy.)

3.6   Speaking skills
e.g. learning through group work.

3.6.1   Discussion skills
questioning
responding
prompting
timing input
exemplifying
obtaining a sense of 'audience'

3.6.2   Debating skills
proposing an idea
opposing an idea
amending: adding
summarizing

3.7   Note-taking and note-making

3.7.1   Purposes
e.g.
(i) notes from textbooks, background reading,
lectures, moving-pictures
(ii) notes for essays; projects; lab reports; revision.

3.7.2   Techniques
(a) choosing a title—defining what notes are for and
source of information
(b) selecting the facts—what to put in and in what order

(c) abbreviations and messages
　　　shortening sentences and words
　　　using symbols
(d) layout of notes (linear)
　　　main points
　　　sub-points
　　　linking
　　　numbering and lettering
　　　underlining
　　　colour
(e) layout of notes in diagrams (pattern-notes)
　　　word association
　　　using images
　　　use of colour/large and small print
　　　underlining/numbering and lettering
(f) noting sources and selecting and acknowledging
　　　quotations
(g) storage and retrieval systems
　　　files
　　　box files
　　　numbering systems and colour coding
　　　indexes

3.8　Using information

3.8.1　*Assessing accuracy of sources*
　　　(primary and secondary sources)

3.8.2　*Distinguishing between fact and opinion*

3.8.3　*Distinguishing between relevant and irrelevant*
　　　information

3.8.4　*Comparing information from different sources*

3.8.5　*Relating information to one's own existing knowledge*
　　　and experience

3.8.6　*Evaluating opinion in relation to supporting information*

3.8.7　*Ordering information for a specific purpose*
　　　e.g. making generalizations
　　　　　offering explanations
　　　　　constructing hypotheses.

3.9 Presenting information

3.9.1 *Kinds of writing*
essays
projects
diaries
reports
notices
letters and memoranda
lists
notes
articles
manuals and guides

3.9.2 *Writing skills*
Writing techniques
(a) organizing notes
(b) structuring essays and reports
 use of headings
 beginnings and ends
 paragraphing
 references and footnotes
 summaries and abstracts
(c) presenting illustrative materials
 charts and diagrams
 tables
 maps, sketches, plans, etc.
(d) writing purposes
 (i) presenting facts
 (ii) presenting ideas
 (iii) presenting observations

3.9.3 *Other forms of presentation*
(a) making tapes
(b) presenting slides/photographic/visual material
(c) making posters/charts, etc.
(d) preparing video-tapes
(e) spoken presenting/verbal reports.

3.10 Self-appraisal

3.10.1 *Comparing finished product with initial intention*

3.10.2 Identifying strengths/weaknesses
    (a) what learnt
    (b) what skills used
    (c) what improvements needed
    (d) strategies for improvement.

3.11   Examination techniques

3.11.1 Self-organization
    (a) planning revision time
    (b) knowing examination timetable and examination requirements
    (c) organizing revision facilities
    (d) organizing length of study period.

3.11.2 Revision and review
    reviewing units of work at frequent intervals
    condensing and systematizing notes
    memory techniques e.g. aides to memory; short-term and long-term memory transference
    using past papers and timed answers.

3.11.3 Taking examinations
    (a) reading examination paper and following instructions
    (b) selecting appropriate questions
    (c) understanding 'type' of question and terms of question
    (d) planning time in examination
    (e) planning answers
    (f) presenting and illustrating answers
    (g) multiple choice.

4 *The implications of a whole school policy on study skills*

    (a) A whole school approach to study skills necessitates the involvement of all staff in the awareness, identification, and development of strategies to overcome learning difficulties. The study skills checklist can only become a meaningful reality if analysed by departments. The result of the analysis should sensitize staff to the pupils' needs and to the contributions that staff can make to overcome pupils' learning difficulties.

(b) A three-phase approach to the development of a study skills programme is proposed:
  (i) awareness by staff of the value of introducing study skills' strategies;
  (ii) identifying the staff training needs to acquire an understanding of the strategies;
  (iii) implementing the strategies within the subject curriculum.
(c) Implementation of a whole school policy on study skills should proceed at a rate which is neither too rapid nor too protracted. Combined efforts must be applied by all staff to monitor developments in students' learning activities which indicate incremental improvement in learning-to-learn skills over their school careers.

5 *Proposals*

It is proposed that:
(a) Departments are requested to consider the use of the framework offered in Appendix 'A' to analyse a section of the content of their teacing and learning programmes and to indicate the skills required by pupils in the areas covered.
(b) School-focussed INSET workshops be arranged which are interdepartmental to discuss the nature of the skills, strategies, and available resources to facilitate implementation.
(c) Monitoring procedures be established to track each pupil's skill attainment at intervals in both departmental and pastoral programmes. A suitable developmental profile should be designed.

References

1 Department of Education and Science *Aspects of secondary education in England* (HMSO 1979)
2 Irving A. (ed) *Starting to teach study skills* (Arnold 1982)
3 Department of Education and Science *Mixed ability work in comprehensive schools* (HMSO 1978)
4 Department of Education and Science *Gifted children in Middle and Comprehensive Secondary Schools* (HMSO 1978)
5 Shayer M. and Adey P. *Towards a Science of Science Teaching* (Heinemann Educational Books 1981)
6 Kelly A. *The Missing Half* (Manchester University Press 1981)
7 Welch J. *Language policy statements in the ILEA* (ILEA 1979)
8 Sutton C. *Communicating in the Classroom* (Hodder and Stoughton 1981)

Index